A Guide to Megalithic Ireland

BY THE SAME AUTHOR:

Astral Doorways

The Dictionary of Mind, Body and Spirit
(with Eileen Campbell)

Discover Astral Projection

Discover Reincarnation

Experimental Magic

Mindreach

Nostradamus: Visions of the Future

Reincarnation

A Guide to Megalithic Ireland

J. H. BRENNAN

Aquarian/Thorsons
An Imprint of HarperCollins*Publishers*

The Aquarian Press
An Imprint of HarperCollins*Publishers*
77-85 Fulham Palace Road,
Hammersmith, London W6 8JB
1160 Battery Street
San Francisco, California 94111-1213

Published by The Aquarian Press 1994
1 3 5 7 9 10 8 6 4 2

A catalogue record for this book
is available from the British Library

ISBN 1 85538 270 9

Phototypeset by Harper Phototypesetters Limited,
Northampton, England
Printed in Great Britain by
HarperCollinsManufacturing Glasgow

ILLUSTRATION CREDITS

Photographs: The Slide File (figs. 1, 2, 18, 21, 24, 26), Don Sutton Photo Library (fig. 3), Kenneth McNally (figs. 4, 5, 6, 7, 8, 9, 10, 11, 12, 14, 15, 19, 20, 22, 23), The Office of Public Works, Ireland (figs. 13, 16, 25, 27, 29, 31), Anthony Weir/Janet & Colin Bord (fig. 17), Bord Failte/Irish Tourist Board (fig. 28, 30).

What to Look for illustrations: Gillian March
Technical Illustrations: Val Barclay

Contents

Introduction

Ten thousand years ago or more, Middle Stone Age hunters first penetrated the dense woodland that was ancient Ireland. They were nomads who followed the game in a seasonal pattern and they left their mark in tiny temporary campsites such as that found in recent years at Lough Boora in County Offaly.

Excavations show the remnants of round houses constructed of interwoven branches and covered with sods of earth. The people who lived in them probably originated in the Isle of Man, Scotland, north-west England or (although a little less likely) Wales. They came to Ireland attracted by the abundance of a vital raw material - flint. They killed boar in the forest and fished salmon from the rivers. They had the country to themselves for close on 3,000 years.

Times changed with the advent of the New Stone Age with a wave of farming people spreading west from Europe. They were a settled race, as farmers have to be, and their homes were substantially more sophisticated than those of their predecessors. Some had stone foundations. Walls were of planks or wattle and daub (essentially clay reinforced with branches). Roofs were probably thatched with reed or straw. It was a style of architecture destined to last almost up to modern times - there is still many a thatched cottage in Ireland which has part, or all, of its walls constructed from wattle and daub.

Unlike their European counterparts, the farmers did not drift into village communities, but instead established isolated family settlements. They built stone walls to pen their livestock and left one another well alone. Their lives were lived before changing climate caused the bogs to form in Ireland.

This orthodox archaeological picture of Irish prehistory is reflected in Irish myth. The ancient sagas tell of sturdy, dark-haired (sometimes dark-skinned) peoples called the Fomor and the Fir Bolg (see boxed reference on page 36) who inhabited the forest wilderness. Both were replaced - following bloody battles - by handsome, fair-skinned invaders known as the Tuatha Dé Danaan. (See boxed reference on page 116.)

The later Celts were so impressed by the Tuatha Dé Danaan that they worshipped them as gods - an attitude that survived into the 15th Century. If, as some scholars believed, the Fir Bolg came from Greece, the Tuatha were thought to come from heaven. They were followers of the goddess Danu, a race of mystics and magicians, capable of creating marvels.

Among the marvels created by the settled farmers of prehistoric Ireland were the country's megalithic monuments. *Megalith* comes from the Greek and means 'great stone'. There are many different types of megalithic monument to be found in Ireland, ranging from single pillarstones to imposing dolmens.

Archaeologists are confident in their use of the term 'tomb' to describe certain megalithic formations. (I have used classical terms like 'portal tomb', 'court tomb' or 'cemetery site' for the sake of uniformity.) But there are mysteries remaining about the actual purpose of the constructions.

There is no doubt at all that burials took place in some of them, although the remains were often cremated first. Nor is there much doubt that some dolmens were originally covered by mounds. But bones placed in court tombs are often separated, suggesting they might once have been buried elsewhere and placed in the court tomb later. The same might be said for other megalithic 'tomb' types as well, many of which show no sign of ever having anything buried (or reburied) in them at all.

For this reason, even the most conservative of archaeologists have postulated the possibility that the chambered structures - particularly those of large and complex architecture - were religious ritual sites used for occasional burials of important people precisely because they had become hallowed ground.

This makes more sense than the straightforward graveyard hypothesis. The great passage 'tombs' at Knowth are heavily decorated, suggesting religious or artistic feeling. The most famous passage tomb of all, Newgrange, is a precise piece of engineering designed to catch a single ray of sunlight on the Winter Solstice.

Some pillarstones mark a cist grave - or was the burial site deliberately chosen to be close to the stone? Many mark nothing at all, so far as anyone can discover. Stone circles, by and large, have no connection with death, cremation or burial. To add to the problem, there are ring forts which, manifestly, were never used as forts - they are too far from water and archaeological investigation indicates they were never actually inhabited.

Forts which seem certainly to have been used as forts - like the imposing structures on the Aran Islands - have their own mysteries. Some of them are set behind massive stone barricades. But what did the barricades protect against? The stones are set too far apart to halt human invaders. They might frustrate cavalry . . . except that there were no horses in Ireland at the time they were built.

Martin Brennan, an American artist and author, made careful measurements of the megalithic monuments richly strewn along the Boyne Valley and concluded they were astronomically aligned, the only surviving remnants of an Irish Golden Age in which the people were obsessed by sun-dialling.

His theory receives support from the work of Professor Alexander Thom, who measured stone circles and other megaliths throughout Britain and in France. Thom found the 'circles' were not circular, but were built to a consistent measure (which he named the 'megalithic yard') and astronomically aligned. They were, he concluded, functioning lunar observatories capable of predicting, among other astronomical phenomena, lunar eclipses.

Professor Thom did not, so far as I am aware, examine Irish sites, but it seems likely that his findings would apply equally to monuments in this country.

So too would the findings of dowsers like Guy Underwood and Havelock Fidler, who discovered experimentally that many megalithic sites align with underground water courses and lines of geodesic energy.

Followers of the late Alfred Watkins, author of the much-reprinted *The Old Straight Track*, claim that many megalithic sites in Britain fall on straight lines called *leys*. This certainly holds true for Ireland as a little time with an ordnance survey map will confirm.

Discovering the peculiarities of megalithic sites highlights their mysteries but does not solve them. One might accept that Stone Age farmers were dowsers, but the idea that they were also sophisticated astronomers seems far-fetched ... except that their megalithic monuments show they must have been. The puzzle is what good it did them. The prediction of lunar eclipses, impressive though it may be, does not help you fatten livestock or harvest corn.

To the mystery of ancient minds must be added the mystery of ancient muscle. The capstone at Browne's Hill Dolmen in County Carlow is estimated to weigh a hundred tons. How was it manoeuvred on top of its uprights by a sparse, scattered farming community that did not have the wheel or the horse? Even the picture of sweating men chanting 'Two-six *heave!*' does not make sense: you can only get so many men around a block of stone before they start tripping one another up.

The construction of megalithic monuments was no localised phenomenon. There are an estimated 1,200 sites in Ireland alone, representing a cultural investment of energy so enormous it almost defies imagination. How was it planned? How was it organised? How was it maintained generation after generation?

And if the *how* is difficult to answer, the *why* is more difficult still. Why did the people of the Stone Age set stones to mark water courses they did not tap? Why were they so concerned to predict lunar eclipses that have no practical importance to farmers? Why did they set so many of their megaliths in straight lines over hundreds of miles of countryside?

The speculative literature on just these questions is enormous. The megaliths are an energy grid used by flying saucers. The megaliths mark meeting points of the Fairy Kingdom and our own world. The megaliths are orgone accumulators used to heal whole tribes. The megaliths generate a subtle energy which ensures fertility of plant and soil. But the definitive answer has yet to be given. This, in itself, is an excellent reason for visiting Ireland's megalithic sites and examining the mystery first hand.

You might be the one to solve it.

How To Use This Guide

This Guide is designed as a handbook for anyone who wishes to investigate those megalithic sites located in the Republic of Ireland. Sites are generally listed alphabetically by their nearest city, town or village to allow for easy reference when you find yourself in a particular area and wish to find local megaliths. The sites themselves are listed by distance from the specific centre, closest first.

Two notable exceptions to the listing by town are Newgrange and Tara, both of which are so well known that I have given them separate listings under their own names. The Newgrange listing actually covers the entire megalithic complex along that area of the Boyne Valley and incorporates material on the great sites of Knowth and Dowth. Site names and classifications are shown in **bold** type.

There is a comprehensive Index at the end of the book which is particularly useful as a cross-reference by county and townland. It should also prove useful in tracking down the mythological associations with various sites.

Getting to the sites is not always easy. Some are signposted as ancient monuments, but the majority are not and many lie across fields or up mountain slopes without so much as a trackway to them. I live in Ireland and have visited a great many megalithic sites personally, but with literally hundreds scattered across the country, it would be a life's work to visit them all.

In order to provide a comprehensive guide, I have consequently consulted archaeological surveys and source books, which are usually far more concerned with the nature of the site than how to reach it. The instructions in this guide are as clear as I can make them. Distances are approximate, by road. But nothing beats asking directions when you are in the locality. Local guidebooks, where available, are usually worth consultation in order to fine tune on a megalithic location.

While the focus of the work is on megaliths (i.e. stone constructions) other examples of interesting prehistoric sites which do not necessarily feature great stones - e.g. ring forts - are generally included.

I have also, on a whim, elected to include ogham stones in the listings. Ogham stones are stones inscribed with the linear script of ancient Ireland. They are not contemporary with the dolmens and pillarstones. Indeed they are not even prehistoric, since the earliest of them dates to about the 5th century AD. But I like to feel there is a continuity of tradition here, even though there is not a scrap of evidence to support the idea.

A similar difficulty arises out of the inclusion of ring forts. Where these are earthen structures, they are almost always prehistoric. Where stone has been used in their construction, they are sometimes prehistoric, but can date well into historical times - as late as the end of the first millennium AD. Even here, however, these comparatively modern structures can occupy far more ancient sites. Consequently I have included them.

Boxed entries refer to mythical associations with

the sites or some particularly interesting theory about them. I have slotted them in where appropriate, but since they are not in alphabetical order, it is best to refer to the Index when faced with a mythic allusion which requires expansion.

Finally, it is important to note that, apart from ogham stones and certain ring forts, historical constructions are ignored, although they may gain a passing mention when they form a convenient landmark in finding a particular megalith, or when they are specifically associated with a megalithic site.

This was a necessity of time, space and economy, but it was also a great pity, for Ireland is exceptionally rich in historical sites of all descriptions. If you can, take time to investigate a few of them as well.

What To Look For

There is such a variety of Stone Age monuments that even archaeologists are sometimes confused by their classification. The situation is further complicated in Ireland by the use of local terms such as *rath* which may not be immediately familiar to overseas visitors.

To help you to use the Guide to your best advantage, archaeological and local terms are defined alphabetically in this section and the major megalithic monuments illustrated.

Boulder tomb A comparatively small (usually 2m x 1m x 1m) capstone set on low supporting uprights which scarcely protrude from the ground. They are often associated with **stone circles**, particularly in Counties Cork and Kerry.

Bullaun A hollow in a boulder cut in order to grind grain.

Cairn Literally a pile of stones. The term is used loosely as a generic for structures like passage tombs or dolmens or, more accurately, to describe the stone work of monuments which have, or once had, other elements, such as earthworks, as well.

Caiseal See **Cathair**.

Callatrach See **Cillín.**

Cashel See **Cathair.**

Cathair A stone-built **ring fort** (q.v.).
Ceallúrach See **Cillín.**
Cillín A circular enclosure sometimes mistaken for a small prehistoric **ring fort**, but actually dating from early Christian times. Traditionally, these have been used as burial sites, particularly for unbaptised children, although archaeological investigation suggests this was not their original purpose. Cillíns are very frequently the site of **ogham stones**.
Cist grave A box-like structure of stone slabs in which the corpse, or cremated remains, was placed. Cist graves had no covering except for the earth of the mound in which they were set. Short (usually square) cists date from early to middle Bronze Age. Long cists (about six feet by one and a half feet wide) are later and were known into Christian times.
Cliff fort Semi-circular **ring fort** defended to the rear by the cliff edge on which it is built.
Clochán Houses built with tapering courses of flat stones. Although the method remained in use into modern times, the oldest clocháns - round, beehive structures - date to the Neolithic era.
Court cairn See **Court tomb.**
Court grave See **Court tomb**.
Court tomb A flat-roofed gallery fronted by a semi-circular 'courtyard' marked out by stones. Sometimes these structures are quite complex, with more than one internal chamber.

Crannóg An artificially constructed island on which a house was raised. The name comes from *crann*, a tree, indicating the extensive use of wood in these constructions.

Cromlech See **Portal tomb**.

Cursing stone Any stone traditionally used to generate malevolent spells. Cursing stones are often small, but associated with much larger megaliths. They are usually unmarked, but a few are **hole stones** (q.v.).

Dallán See **Pillarstone**.

Dolmen See **Portal tomb**. The term is Scandinavian and means 'stone table'.

Fougous See **Souterrain.**

Gallán See **Pillarstone**.

Glacial erratic A boulder or similar large stone deposited by retreating glaciers at the end of the Ice Age. The importance of such stones to megalith hunters is that they can often give the impression of having been artificially placed in a particular site.

Henge See **Stone circle**.

Hill fort Ring fort (q.v.) on a hilltop or mountainside location.

Hole stone A megalith, sometimes standing alone, sometimes associated with a more complex structure, which is distinguished by having a hole through it. Such stones are often associated with healing and fertility. Where size permitted, babies and small children were often passed through the holes in an attempt to cure their diseases right up to modern times.

Horned cairn See **Court tomb**.

Kitchen midden See **Midden**.

Liagán See **Pillarstone**.

Lios See **Rath**.

Long barrow A generic to describe structures like **court tombs** and **passage tombs.** Essentially any megalithic tomb which was composed of a mound and passage. The term 'long barrow' is far more prevalent in Britain than in Ireland.

Menhir See **Pillarstone**.

Midden Neolithic (and later) refuse site.

Monolith See **Pillarstone**.

Motte A flat-topped earthwork mound, indicating the remains of a castle. Although obviously not prehistoric, such mounds are sometimes built on more ancient structures. Where there is some indication that this may have been the case, mottes are included in this Guide.

Ogham stone A stone, often upright, inscribed in the lines and notches of the early Irish ogham script. The inscriptions are usually commemorative, giving the name of an individual and recent ancestors.

Orthostat A large upright stone, differentiated from a pillarstone in that it will usually form part of a larger structure, such as a court tomb.

Outlier A megalithic feature, usually a standing stone, which lies outside the boundaries of the main monument.

Passage tomb A passage leading into a central chamber, usually set within a mound.

Pillarstone Single upright stones, sometimes set within the earthwork of a ring fort, sometimes forming part of a stone circle, sometimes located without reference to any obvious geographical feature.

Portal tomb Three or more upright stones supporting a capstone.

Promontory fort Defensive system constructed across the neck of a peninsula or sometimes across a mountain spur.

Rath An earthen **ring fort** (q.v.).

Ring fort A circular enclosure surrounded by an earthwork bank and ditch, or sometimes a stone rampart.

Souterrain An artificial cave or passage cut into clay or rock, often with stone-faced walls and roof. In Ireland, the majority of souterrains are associated with forts.

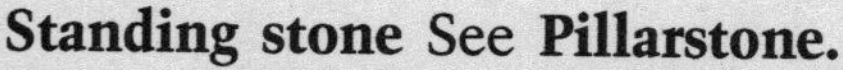

Standing stone See **Pillarstone.**

Stone alignments Groups of **standing stones** (q.v.) arranged in one or more straight lines. This form is very rare in Ireland.

Stone circles Groups of standing stones arranged in a (roughly) circular pattern, often with one or more outliers.

Tóchar See **togher**.

Togher An ancient roadway.

Tumulus An earthen mound, sometimes artificial.

Wag See **Souterrain.**

Wedge tomb A passage set into a wedge-shaped mound which tapers along its length. Usually dated as Bronze Age.

Weem See **Souterrain.**

Where To Find Them

The maps which follow show the distribution, by type, of the more interesting Irish megalithic monuments. They are followed by a key map showing the locations of the major sites (of any type) which are recommended for visiting.

Distribution of court tombs

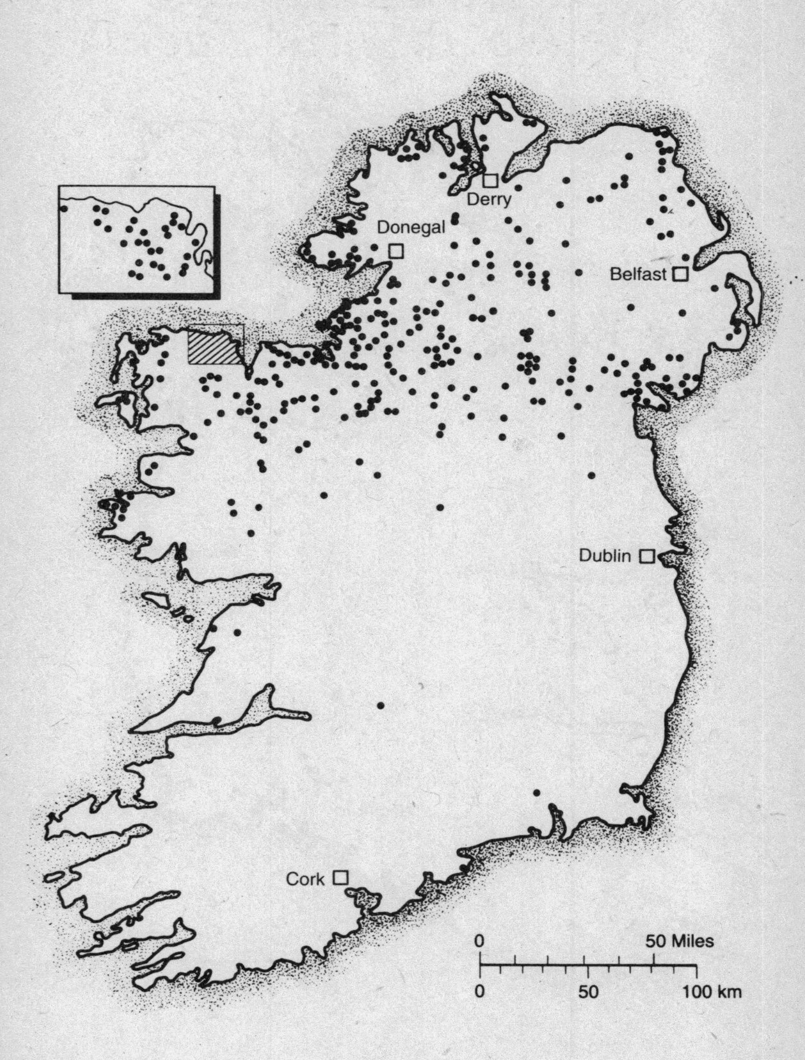

Distribution of portal tombs (dolmens)

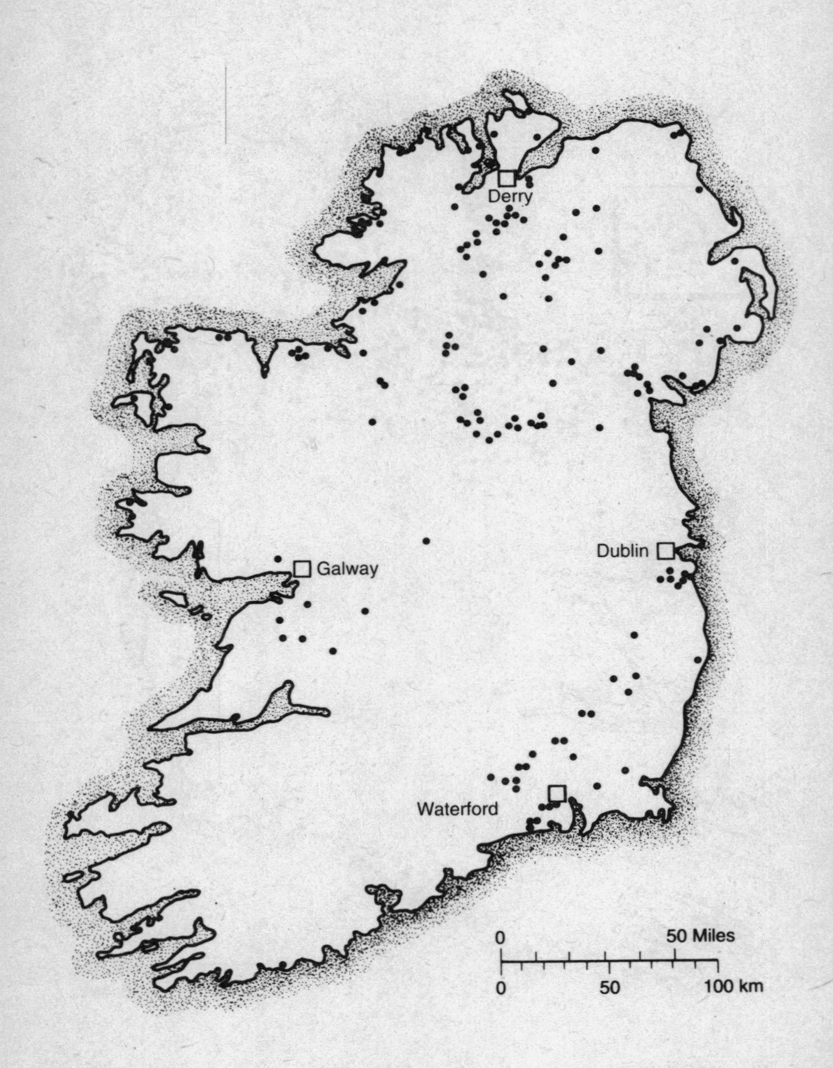

Distribution of passage tombs

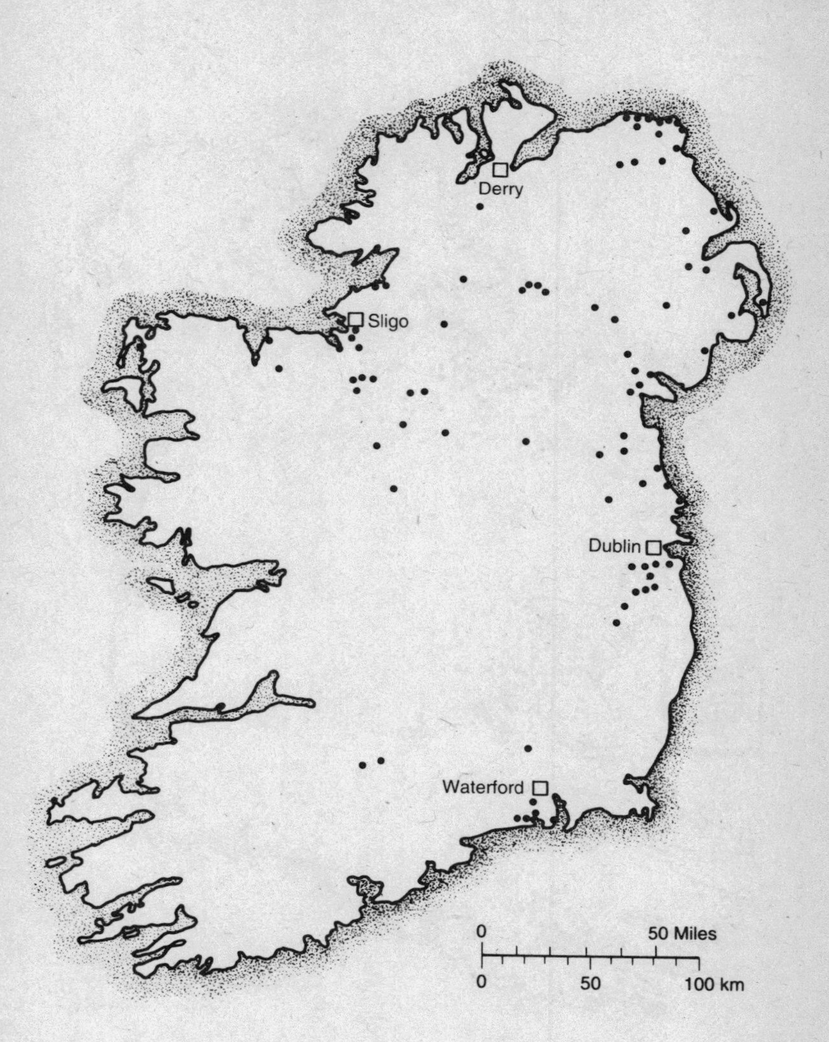

Distribution of wedge tombs

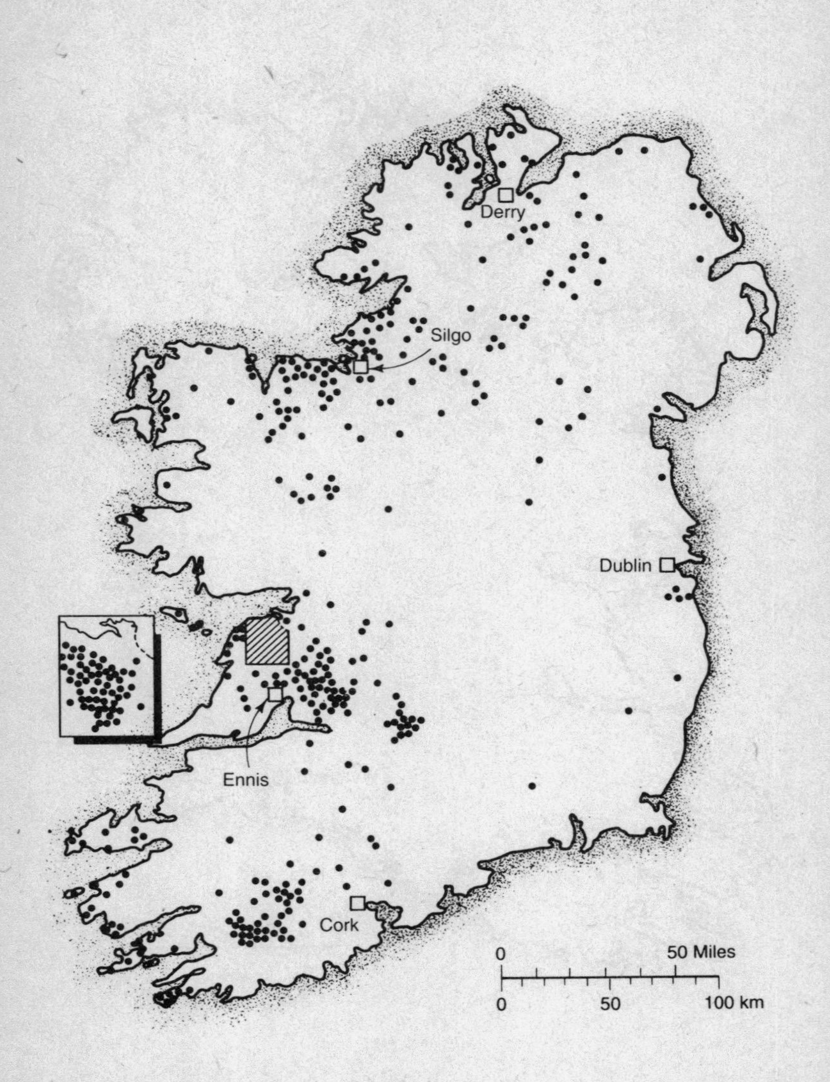

Distribution of stone circles

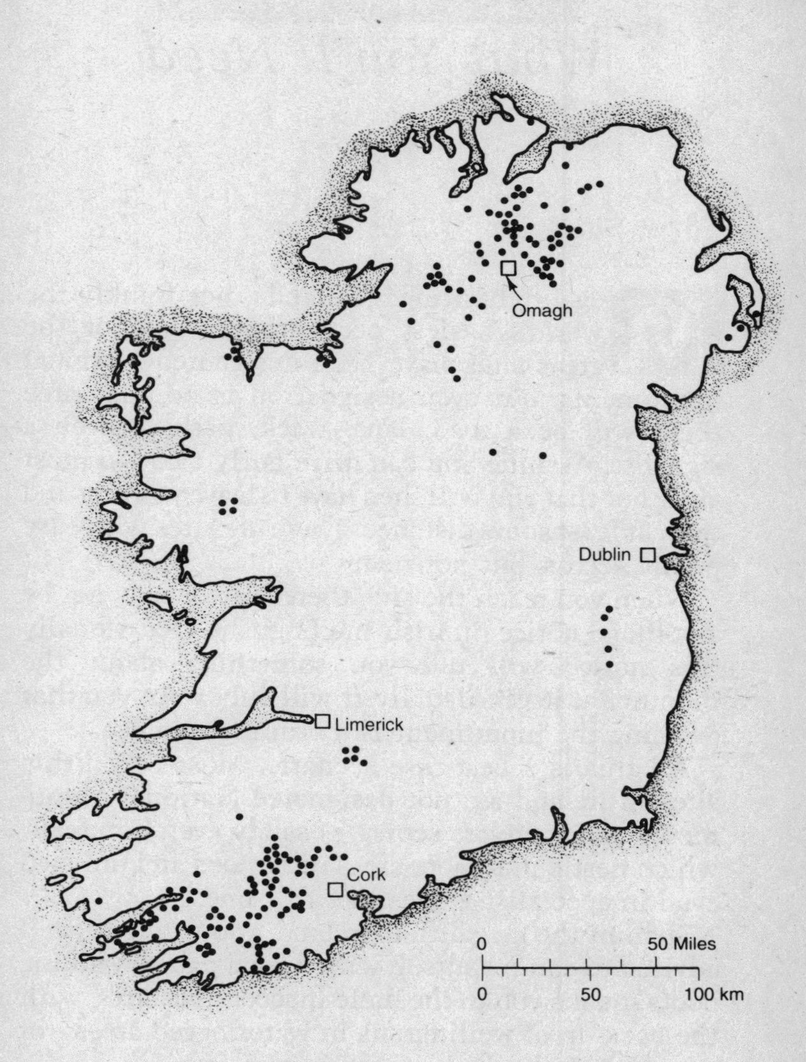

What You'll Need

Megalith hunting in Ireland is not, frankly, the world's easiest occupation. Many of the great sites have been designated National Monuments, but even designation is no guarantee there will be a road, lane, track, path or even a signpost. Assume you can drive fairly close to most sites, but that you will then have to leave your car and walk at least some distance. There *are* sites with easy public access, but not many.

When you reach the site, there may or may not be an official notice (in Irish and English). Occasionally this notice will tell you something about the monument itself. Usually, it will only warn you that defacing the monument is a criminal offence.

All this is a best-case scenario. Most megalithic sites in Ireland are not designated National Monuments and there are scores, possibly even hundreds, which nestle in remote areas unnoticed and unlisted even in specialist guides like this one.

To hunt the megalith in Ireland, you would be well advised to equip yourself with a good pair of walking boots to take you to the more inaccessible sites, with the back-up of wellingtons in waterlogged areas - of which, in Ireland, there are quite a few.

In the more popular tourist areas, local guides and maps are always well worth buying, since they will often help you locate sites which might otherwise be overlooked. In districts where tourism is not an obvious industry, an Ordnance Survey map can be an excellent investment.

Many gift shops, newsagents, book shops and filling stations carry the half inch touring maps relevant to their area - there are 25 in all, published by the Ordnance Survey of Ireland, which combine to cover the whole country. The numbered references in this Guide are taken from these sheets. (See the section on How to Locate The Sites, immediately following this one, for instructions on how to interpret them.)

There is also available a beautifully produced and very useful specialist map of monastic sites in Ireland, but at the time of writing there is nothing comparable on megaliths. The monastic map is worth having, however, due to the commonplace Christian practice of taking over ancient pagan sites.

If you are really serious about your megalith hunting, it is well worth making the Ordnance Survey your first port of call. The office is located in the Phoenix Park in Dublin and for a reasonable fee you can buy photocopies of very large scale maps relating to specific areas of local interest.

These maps can be an absolute goldmine for the megalith hunter since they often show sites that are literally unlisted anywhere else. But there are drawbacks.

The first is the question of scale. While it is the large scale that makes these maps so useful, that same scale means you may have to purchase several maps to cover the full extent of the area that interests you. While the fee per map is modest, your investment can quickly mount up.

The next is the question of quality. You are *not* buying the precision printing and clarity of a published map, merely a copy of an official record. What you get is a black and white document which makes an excellent working tool, but can sometimes be a little difficult to read.

The last is the question of age. Ordnance survey is ongoing work and the authorities are updating maps all the time, but the fact remains that some of the large scale maps you buy will be copies of originals dating back to the British occupation. This is not all bad news: the British had a huge respect for megalithic sites and were very conscientious in recording them. However, not all sites shown remain today and those that do are not always as accessible as they were. Once, for example, I went in search of a stone circle marked on a large-scale Ordnance Survey copy only to find that what was shown as open farmland was now a Forestry Commission fir plantation. It took almost an afternoon to find the remains of the circle, now scarcely discernible as a megalithic site at all.

Fortunately, deliberate damage to the old sites is rare in Ireland - and for an interesting reason. Throughout the country, particularly in the rural areas, they are associated with the Fairy Folk and it is widely believed that interference with a site will lead to bad luck.

This theory is taken very seriously indeed. Just two years ago, in County Kildare, I heard the story of a farmer unwise enough to bulldoze an ancient rath in order to plant corn. The fury of the Fairy Folk would have done justice to a Hammer film. At harvest time his corn caught mysteriously alight, the fire swept through his fields to destroy not only his crops, but eventually to burn down his farmhouse with the loss of his wife and children.

Incidents of this sort feed the old folk beliefs, which are further reinforced by the curious fact that thorn bushes (also strongly associated with the Fairy Folk in Ireland) often grow on or near megalithic sites.

The overall result is that the great stones are generally revered or feared in Ireland and consequently left undisturbed. It is quite common to see ploughing circumvent a mid-field rath and while stones at a few sites have been cannibalised for building (Newgrange was a notable example) this sort of thoughtless vandalism is rare.

One of the great joys of megalith hunting is finding a hitherto undiscovered site. This is still possible in Ireland where archaeologists readily admit to the likelihood that forgotten monuments exist. But finding them is not a question of exploring uncharted territory. Rather, it is a question of differentiating between a man-made structure and a natural distribution of stones.

This is not always easy. The typical capstone and uprights of a portal tomb are distinctive enough, but a glacial erratic can easily be mistaken for a pillarstone and there are boulder-strewn areas which could easily disguise an entire stone circle. Worse still, these are exactly the areas where the likelihood of a prehistoric site is greatest - the raw materials are close to hand.

One possible way of differentiating between the natural and the man-made is to make use of the fascinating discovery by Professor Alexander Thom that the megalith builders made use of a standard unit of measurement - the so-called 'megalithic yard'.

Thom's discovery was made in Britain, and while his findings have yet to be confirmed in any large-scale Irish survey there remains a strong probability that they are applicable here as well. If so, you have only to make yourself a 'megalithic yardstick' of 2.72 feet - string knotted at 2.72 feet intervals is a convenient form of the instrument - and measure your suspect site. If the stones are set to this ancient standard, they were probably sited deliberately. If not, the chances are you are dealing with erratics.

(I used this technique in an attempt to test P.A. O'Síocháin's claim that there were the remains of a stone circle in a field below the Athgreany Piper's Stones in County Wicklow. Several of them did indeed pass the megalithic yard test.)

Overall then, your equipment list should include walking shoes, wellingtons, local maps and a megalithic yardstick. A camera is a good if obvious idea, as is a pair of binoculars. Less obvious are paper and pencil to take rubbings of megalithic scribings. These are sometimes so weathered that it is virtually impossible to get them to show up in a photograph without specialist lighting and equipment.

Finally, since you will presumably be examining ogham (pronounced *ohm*) stones in your wanderings, the following key to the ogham alphabet may be of interest:

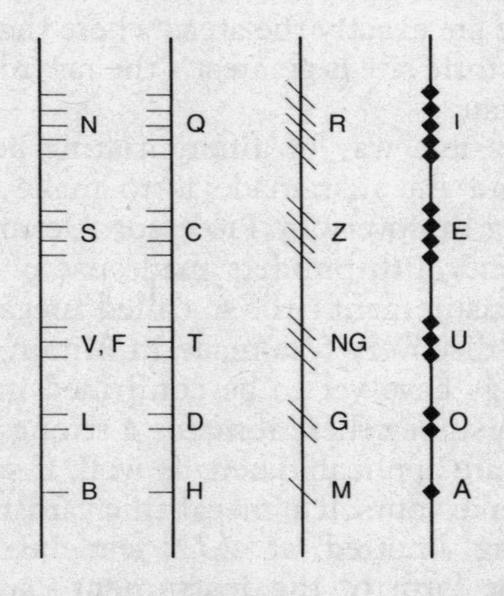

How To Locate the Sites

Site references listed in this Guide relate to the Irish National Grid which divides the island into 25 100-kilometer square zones. Each zone is officially identified by a letter of the alphabet. (The letter 'I' is the one left out.) You can use the Grid to find your way through any of the 25 half-inch touring maps published by the Ordnance Survey. These maps do *not* coincide with Grid zones and are consequently designated by number and locality.

Each Grid reference listed in this Guide takes the form of an alphabet letter followed by four figures. The alphabet letter obviously refers to its zone on the national grid. The figures require a bit of explanation.

You locate any given site with reference to the south-west corner of the Grid zone in which it lies. The first two figures in your Grid reference are the measurement eastwards. The last two are the measurement northwards. So if you had, for example, the reference number **T 12 34** on a site, it would mean the site lies in Grid zone T, twelve kilometers east of the south-west corner and thirty-four kilometers north.

The best way to get the hang of this is to try it out using an actual map. Assume you are trying to find site **S 69 65**, then proceed as follows:

First, check the alphabet letter **S** against the

How To Locate the Sites

National Grid illustration. This gives you the broad zone in which the site lies.

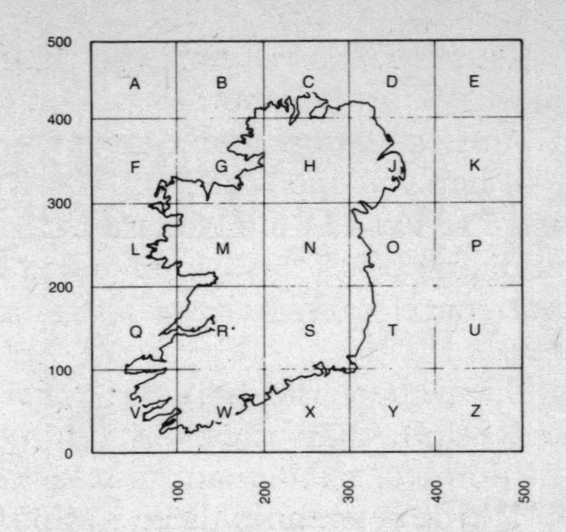

Next, find the relevant half-inch Ordnance Survey sheet by referring to the following diagram:

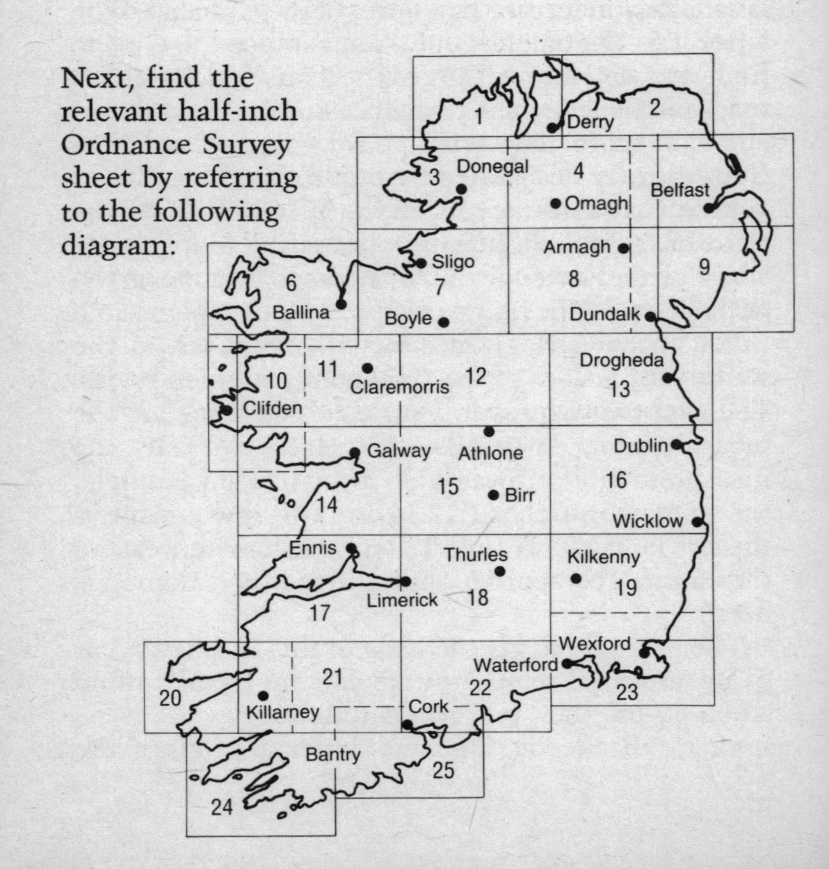

This indicates that the half-inch map you're looking for is Map 19, which covers portions of Counties Carlow and Wexford.

When you open the map, you will find it is divided into squares. Each square is a 10-kilometer subdivision of the National Grid. The vertical and horizontal lines of the subdivisions are numbered 00 to 90.

If you check the margins of your half-inch map, you will find that these 10-kilometer squares have 1-kilometer subdivision markings along the edges.

To find your sample site **S 69 65,** look along the top horizontal margin of your map until you see the figure 60. Count to your right (i.e. eastward) along the single kilometer subdivisions until you reach 69.

Now go to the left hand vertical margin and again look for the figure 60. When you find it, count upwards (i.e. north) a further five of the kilometer subdivisions to reach 65. Draw a line across *right* from your north measurement and a line *down* from your east measurement. Where the two cross, you will find your site. (In this example, you will know you have done it right if the lines cross at Leighlinbridge.)

In the field, the reference pinpoints the site to within one square kilometer. If you get that close and still cannot find it, ask locally for directions.

The Guide

Abbey, County Galway

(Sheet 15) There are two **wedge tombs** and a **portal tomb** at Marble Hill (M 69 03) about three and a half miles west-south-west of this little town.

Achill, County Mayo

(Sheet 6) Achill is a large rugged island off the Mayo coast, accessible by a bridge which crosses Achill Sound. In this area of outstanding natural beauty you need travel only about six miles to reach Slievemore – the name means Great Mountain – a 2,200 foot mass rising sharply from the ocean.

From the village of Keel, (the name means a narrow place, such as a valley or river) take the road to the deserted village (ruins of a pre-Famine settlement on the lower slopes of the mountain) but take the Atlantic Drive turn-off before you reach it. On this road is a signpost designated 'Megalithic Tomb', pointing to a narrow walkway up the mountain.

It is a steep climb, but you can always pretend to admire the stunning view when you get breathless. It takes you to the Keel East **Giant's Grave**, (F 64 07) a **horned cairn** in only a reasonable state of preservation.

According to local guide books, there are five further **court tombs** on the southern slope of the mountain and another near the shore of the lake

below, but in two days of searching I was able to find only one of these, in a field behind a local hotel.

Anascaul, County Kerry

(Sheet 20) Three interesting sites lie within a few miles of this hamlet on the Tralee-Dingle road. About one and a quarter miles east, in the townland of Ballintermon (Q 62 02) you will find an **ogham** stone. Two miles north-west in Knockane is what is left of a large tumulus which houses a **cist grave** (Q 58 03). Nearby, to the south-east, is a **boulder** on which has been inscribed a cross. Three miles north-north-east there is a second **ogham** stone which forms part of the east gable of a house in Ballinahunt (Q 61 06).

Aran Islands, County Galway

(Sheet 14) You can reach the three Aran Islands – Inishmore, Inishmaan and Inisheer – by boat or air. Aran knitwear is world famous and has a little-known connection with Ireland's prehistoric past in that elements of the traditional patterns can be found on ancient megaliths, suggesting great antiquity for the designs.

Monastic settlement dates back to Saint Éanna in the 6th century AD but for prehistory buffs the real interest must lie in the dry-stone forts and other monuments believed locally to have been built by the semi-legendary Fir Bolg. The Fir Bolg were Ireland's aboriginal inhabitants (see boxed reference on page 36) subsequently displaced by the Tuatha Dé Danaan invaders. (See boxed reference on page 116.) The most interesting remnants of Fir Bolg occupation are to be found on Inishmore and Inishmaan, although all three islands have a multitude of prehistoric and early Christian sites. If you possibly can, pull on a pair of stout boots and spend a day or two exploring. If you positively must be selective, the following really should not be missed:

Inishmaan

Visit Moher (the first village to the west of the landing place) and you are within 300 yards of a collapsed **wedge tomb** to the north-north-east. About 400 yards west of Ballinlisheen village in the centre of the island is the spectacular oval **stone fort** of **Dún Conchubhair** (L 93 04). This fort occupies the highest ground on the island, measuring about 50 x 27m with a massive terrace wall. There is an outer wall which guards three sides of the oval then links with the inner structure. There has been considerable restoration work carried out on the rampart and on the interior hut sites.

Inishmore

Find the village of Oghil. To the east of the old lighthouse nearby lies **Oghil fort** (L 87 10) which has two concentric ramparts, one of them terraced. There are the remains of two **clocháns** within the enclosure.

Cowrugh village is within easy walking distance of Oghil. From there, go south to discover the ruined **Clochán a' Phúca** (the Clochán of the Spirits) and south-west for an interesting wedge tomb.

From Cowrugh, it is only about two miles to Kilmurvy village. From Kilmurvy go south-west until you reach the cliff where you will find **Dún Aonghus**, a fort (L 81 09) which covers fully 11 acres and is generally recognised as one of the finest prehistoric monuments in Europe.

The fort was partially restored in the late 19th century and its three concentric enclosures are, to say the least, spectacular. Climb the ramparts of the innermost enclosure for an amazing view of the whole island and, indeed, the Connemara coast. The name Dún Aonghus reflects the link with the Fir

Bolg (see boxed reference below). According to the Medieval legend, Aonghus was one of their chieftains.

You will find Onaght village just under two miles north-west of Kilmurvy. Wander just half a mile south-south-east to find **Dún Onaght**, (L 81 11) another massive stone **ring fort**. This one has been restored as well and features a terraced rampart.

About two miles south-east of Onaght is Killeany village. If you take to the cliffs from Killeany, you will find the great **promontory fort** of **Dubh Cathair** (L 80 10) a mile and a half to the west. There is some evidence to suggest this may be the oldest fort on the island. There is a huge drystone wall rising to a height of eighteen feet in places. It is terraced on the inside, while there are indications of chevaux de frise on the outside. A series of stone huts nestles close to the

Fir Bolg

The Fir Bolg were the third group of invaders to enter Ireland, arriving just 600 years after the Biblical Flood. They were ruled by King Eochy MacEirc whose marriage to the fair Tailtiu brought him a palace as part of her dowry.

Tailtiu was so popular that the annual Lughnasa Fair (named for the Sun God Lugh) was held over her grave at Teltown in County Meath for many years - including a brief revival in the present century.

A subsequent wave of invaders, the mystical Tuatha Dé Danaan, overcame the Fir Bolg in a series of bloody battles, but graciously allowed the 'bag men' - the literal translation of Fir Bolg - to settle in the West of Ireland.

Legend has it that the Fir Bolg were the first to introduce iron spearheads into Ireland. An interesting development if true, since ancient lore avers that only iron could harm the fairy folk.

curved wall. There used to be an entrance gate, but this fell into the sea in the early years of the 19th century when a portion of the cliff collapsed.

The Arans are a paradise for anyone interested in prehistoric and early Christian sites. Spectacular though they are, the few described above scarcely scratch the surface of the many, many delights. The islands themselves are small - as you will have gathered from the short distances between villages - so finding sites is unusually easy.

Ardagh, County Limerick

(Sheet 17) You can see for yourself where Ireland's famed Ardagh Chalice and Ardagh Brooch were discovered in the 19th century by visiting the **ring fort** (R 27 38) at the west end of the village. Although designated as a National Monument, this large fort is overgrown and defaced.

A mile to the north-west of the village is a second **ring fort**, at Ballylin (R 27 39), which is among the very largest of such structures in the country.

Ardfert, County Kerry

(Sheet 20) Travel no more than a mile south-west to find **McKenna's ring fort** (Q 77 20) a site which has the distinction of bridging Ireland's ancient and more recent history. On Good Friday, 1916, the Irish patriot Sir Roger Casement was arrested at the fort. When you have viewed the prehistoric site, visit nearby Banna Strand to see the monument erected to commemorate the arrest (Q 75 22).

Arvagh, County Cavan

(Sheets 12, 8) Three and a half miles north-west of the little village in the townland of Drumhart (Sheet 8) is a **court tomb** (H 24 01).

Athboy, County Meath

(Sheet 13) From this market village on the Trim-Oldcastle road, travel east about a mile to find the **Hill of Ward** (N 73 64). A **ring work** marks the site of an *aonach* or ancient assembly. The meeting convened on Samhain (October 31), suggesting a pre-Christian tradition. In (comparatively) recent times, 13,000 horsemen crowded the area to witness High King Rory O'Connor preside over a national synod in 1168.

Athleague, County Roscommon

(Sheet 12) Castlestrange Demesne, now sadly derelict, lies two miles north-west of Athleague village. Follow the demesne avenue to find **Castlestrange Stone** (M 82 59), a **boulder** of granite which features spiral patterns dating back to at least the Iron Age.

Balbriggan, County Dublin

(Sheet 13) There are a great many sites of substantial historical interest near this busy manufacturing town on the Dublin-Drogheda Road, but perhaps the most fascinating prehistoric monuments are to be found close to The Naul, a tiny hamlet six miles west-south-west on the L89. A mile to the north-west is the townland of Fourknocks where you will find three **tumuli** (O 11 62). One of these is the site of an ancient **cremation trench**, another of a **Bronze Age burial**. The third and most interesting is a cruciform **passage tomb** re-roofed in a modern restoration and featuring a variety of **scribings**.

Ballina, County Mayo

(Sheet 6) Take the road out of Cockle Street three quarters of a mile south-west to find the remnant of a **megalithic tomb** (G 23 18). It is immediately beside the road and signposted as a National Monument.

Ballinafad, County Sligo

(Sheet 7) Four miles north of the village is Castlebaldwin Crossroads, itself an historical site of interest since you will find the 17th-century fortified house of Castle Baldwin there. But the real excitement must be the prehistoric site a little

further on.

Take the road west from the crossroads which forks in about a quarter of a mile. Take the south-west fork which will lead you into the Bricklieve Mountains. A mile and a half further on, fork east then turn south-east where you will find one of the most important - and least known - megalithic monuments in the country.

There are no less than fourteen **chambered cairns** (G 75 12), combining to create a passage tomb cemetery of exceptional interest. One of them, known to archaeologists as Cairn E, consists of the familiar long cairn with a court tomb forecourt joined to a cruciform **passage grave**.

You can get into some of the tombs, but would be well advised to stay outside since all of them are dangerous.

Nearby, in Mullaghfarna, on the north-east spur of the mountain, is the remnants of a **prehistoric village** (G 76 12) of some 70 circular huts ranging in diameter from 20-40 feet. Only the stone footings are left, but the site is worth a visit since it is absolutely unique in Ireland.

Ballinamore, County Leitrim

(Sheet 7) It will come as no surprise to discover that Longstones Townland, a little to the north-east of this village on the Killeshandra-Drumshanbo road, takes its name from a series of **pillarstones** (H 12 12).

These are associated with a further **pillarstone**, a **portal tomb** and the remnants of three **passage tombs** in Fenaghbeg, about a quarter mile north of Ballinamore.

Three miles south-west on the T53 you will find Fenagh, an early monastic site. A further quarter mile south-west in Commons, lie the **Giants' Graves**, a twin **cairn** (H 11 08).

Ballineen, County Cork

(Sheets 25, 24) Ballineen is the twin village of Enniskean. A shade over six miles north-north-west in Capeen West is the **ring fort** of **Cahervaglier** (W 32 63). Within the ring is the remains of a **stone hut** and a **souterrain**.

In Knockane, about half a mile further on, are two **wedge tombs** set one beside the other (W 32 64).

Ballingarry, County Limerick

(Sheet 17) To the east of the village (the name of which means Town of the Garden) rising just short of a thousand feet, is Knockfierna, the Hill of Truth and ancient seat of the god Donn Firinne. **Buacgaill Bréige cairn** (R 45 36) stands on the summit (having been removed and replaced in modern times). Climb the north slope to find the **Giant's Grave**, sometimes known as **Fawha's Grave**, a **wedge tomb** minus its roof.

Ballinrobe, County Mayo

(Sheet 11) Ballinrobe's name means the Town of the River Robe. A mile and a half east of ruined Lough Mask Castle, a 15th-century fortress which itself lies four miles south-west of the town, is **Eochai's Cairn** (M 16 60) named for the mythic leader of the Fir Bolg at the time they arrived in Ireland. (See boxed reference on page 36).

Ballinskelligs, County Kerry

(Sheet 20) The quiet resort village is named for Ballinskelligs Bay on which it stands. Two and a half miles to the north-east, in Meelagulleen, is a ruined **wedge tomb** (V 45 68). Approximately the same distance north of the village, in Killurly Cemetery, is an **ogham stone** (V 41 68).

The Coom mountain-saddle lies three miles

north-west of the village. A mile south of this picturesque spot is a **boulder tomb** with a megalithic **outlier** (V 38 68). A few hundred yards away, eastwards, is a **wedge tomb**.

Ballintogher, County Sligo

(Sheet 7) The name of this hamlet on the Collooney-Manorhamilton road means town of the causeway. Two miles west-south-west leaves you in Carricknagat, a district whose name suggests a rock and contains two **megalithic tombs** (G 73 26).

While in the area, it is worth travelling a further few miles to Lough Dargan, to the south of which is the remains of Castle Dargan, a 15th-century fortification built on the site of an ancient **ring fort** (G 72 28).

A mile north-north-west of Ballintogher is the stone **Castleore ring fort** and the remains of a **court tomb** (G 75 29). There are two further **court tombs** (G 73 29) a mile and a half to the west of Castleore in Carrownagh with a third some 800 yards further west in Arnasbrack.

Ballintra, County Donegal

(Sheet 3) Ballintra is some seven miles south-west of Donegal town, a village on the Ballyshannon-Donegal road. Closest megalithic site to the village is **Giant's Grave**, a ruined **wedge tomb** (G 91 69) about a mile south-west in Ballymagrorty Scotch.

There is rather more to see two and a half miles south-west where you will find **Lurgan Carn** (the Cairn of the Long Hill), an unusual ring enclosure (not necessarily a **ring fort**) which features a **court tomb** (G 89 67).

Ballitore, County Kildare

(Sheet 16) Founded by the Quakers, the village is only

a mile away from the hill of Mullaghmast, celebrated for the massacre there of Irish Chieftains by the English in 1577. There is a **rath** (S 77 95) near the summit where Garret Og, the notorious Wizard Earl of Kildare, is supposed to have been buried. If he really *was* buried there, the tomb did not hold him, for he is reputed to emerge every seven years to ride with his nobles around the Curragh Plain.

(For those as interested in wizards as I am, the Earl's castle still stands at Kilkee - having been magically transformed into an impressive hotel - and visitors can still see evidence of his satanic practices in the pleasantly obscene little carving high up on a rear wall.)

Ballybofey, County Donegal

(Sheet 3) A little more than five miles south-west of this small market town, the N15 road to Donegal passes through Barnesmore Gap. On the southern slope of Croaghconnallagh, the higher of the two mountains, overlooking Lough Mourne, you will find **Cashelnavean** (the Stone Fort of the Fianna), a large stone **ring fort** (H 06 90).

Not far away, to the south of the road at the north-east end of the lough, is the **Giant's Bed**, an interesting **chamber tomb** (H 06 89).

Ballybunnion, County Kerry

(Sheet 17) There are two **promontory forts** close to this popular resort, one south-west of the village, enclosing the remains of Ballybunnion Castle (Q 86 41), while the other lies to the north and encloses the ruins of Pookeenee Castle (Q 86 41).

Ballycastle, County Mayo

(Sheet 6) This little resort at the foot of Ballinglen is an exceptional centre for megalith hunters - there are

The Fianna

The Fianna were the warriors who followed the legendary Irish hero/giant Finn MacCool to death and glory somewhere around 2,000 years ago. (See boxed reference on page 90.)

They were a literate army since an essential qualification for membership was mastery of the 12 forms of Gaelic prose.

Today, they are commemorated in the name of Ireland's largest political party, Fianna Fail, whose leaders may find an object lesson in the fact that the original Fianna grew so arrogant and dictatorial they drew down the wrath of the High King Cairbre, who broke their power at the Battle of Gabhra in AD 284.

no fewer than seven sites within easy reach, some of them of quite extraordinary interest.

The nearest lies less than a mile west-north-west in the townland of Ballyglass. It features a spectacular elliptical **court tomb** (G 09 38) with two segmented galleries. Just over 200 yards south is the remains of a second **court tomb** (G 09 37). At the west end of the first of these tombs, excavations unearthed the foundations of a small timber house dating back to the New Stone Age.

A mile south-east is Rathoonagh, where you will find the remnants of two further **court tombs** (G 11 36) within about half a mile of each other.

Two miles north-west in Doonfeeny Upper, are two (Christian) graveyards. If you ignore the one with the remains of the church, you will find in the other the barest signs of an ancient earthen **ring fort** enclosing a slim **pillarstone** (G 08 39) some 18 feet high.

Just under four miles east-south-east, in Barnhill Upper, you will find yet another **court tomb** (G 14 35).

Six miles north-west is the north-eastern spur of Maumakeogh where at a height of about 500 feet you will find **The Roomeens**, a **court tomb** with a horseshoe court standing in an extensive **Neolithic field system** (G 04 40). The fields were set out before Ireland's bogs were laid down, but you can see remnants of the old stone walls over an area of about four square miles where the bogs have been cut away. There has been some restoration of the tomb itself in that the turf which covered the court has been replaced. Finds at this site included some interesting examples of Neolithic pottery.

Six miles south-south-east, in Ballybeg, is the seventh **court tomb** (G 13 32) in this district.

Finally, if you are prepared to travel ten miles north-west to Belderg townland (F 99 40), you can see the excavated remains of a **Neolithic farm** with a later, Bronze Age **round house**.

Ballyconnel, County Cavan

(Sheet 8) You are in **stone circle** country when you visit this border village at the foot of Slieve Rushen. Just three miles south-west in Killycluggin is a **stone circle** (H 23 16) which used to have an interesting **outlier** featuring Iron Age spiral ornamentation. The stone was, however, broken and its remnants are now in the National Museum in Dublin. The circle itself is 100 feet in diameter and seems to be the remains of a kerb. There was some sort of large megalithic structure in the centre, but only two parallel slabs remain.

A short way to the south-west, in the townland of Kilnavert, you will find a **wedge tomb**, two **pillarstones** and two further **stone circles** (H 23 16). The three neighbouring townlands of Killycluggin, Kilnavert and Lissanover seem once to have been a cult centre dating back to the Bronze Age and

possibly beyond. There are a great many scattered **standing stones** in the district, along with **boulder circles** on hilltops, many of which have the remains of burial chambers within them and a few of which are surrounded by earthen banks. A folk tradition insists that St Patrick overthrew a shrine to the Crom Cruaich (see boxed reference on page 58) here in the form of a **pillarstone** inside a **stone circle**.

Ballycrovane, County Cork

(Sheet 24) Just over 200 yards south-east of the coastguard station at the harbour is a 17-feet tall **pillarstone** (V 65 52) with an **ogham** inscription. Almost certainly this was a prehistoric megalith, perhaps erected to mark the westernmost point of Ireland, with the ogham added at a much later date.

Ballycroy, County Mayo

(Sheet 6) Two miles south-south-west of this tiny village in the townland of Kildun is a **tumulus** which features two **pillarstones** (F 79 07). One of these has a ringed cross cut into its western face.

Ballyferriter, County Kerry

(Sheet 20) Visit the old schoolhouse in this picturesque resort to see local antiquities on display at the Heritage Centre, then travel half a mile south-west to see a **stone circle** (Q 34 03).

Travel three and a half miles east of the town through a collection of historical sites to find a stone **ring fort** (Q 40 04) in Caherdorgan South. There are ruined **stone huts** within the ring. A few hundred yards north-east, in Caherdorgan North is a second **ring fort** enclosing five ruined **clochâns**. Follow the road north to the Chancellor's House (signed as a National Monument), then continue north-east to pass between two **pillarstones**, known locally (and delightfully) as the **Thief Stone** and the **Cow Stone** (Q 40 06). Continue north into Kilmalkedar village and ask directions to the **Alphabet Stone** (Q 40 06), not surprisingly an **ogham stone**.

Ferriter's Cove lies a couple of miles north-west of the village. On its shore, archaeologists unearthed Mesolithic shell **middens** (Q 33 05).

Ballyhaunis, County Mayo

(Sheet 12) Two miles west-north-west of Ballyhaunis in the townland of Island is sited **Braghlaghboy Ogham Stone** (M 47 80). It is situated on a **tumulus** on high ground and is consequently visible for some distance.

Ballyheige, County Kerry

(Sheet 17) Three miles west-north-west from the resort you reach the foot of Trisk Mountain where, in the townland of Glenderry, you will find a cupped **pillarstone** (Q 70 29) on which has been cut a cross, painted red in historical times. There is also a **stone ball** of uncertain provenance which, nonetheless, is reputed to be charmed.

Ballyliffin, County Donegal

(Sheet 1) There are two interesting sites within easy reach of the resort village. Three and a half miles east-north-east in Magheranaul you can find a **wedge tomb** (C 43 50) which has a hole in its portal. North-west of this by about a mile and a quarter in Carrowreagh (often locally called Craignacally) lies **The Altar** (C 42 51) which is not an altar at all, but a **boulder** with prehistoric **scribings**.

Ballymore Eustace, County Kildare

(Sheet 16) Broadleas Common lies one and a half miles south of this attractive Liffeyside village. On a

hilltop there may be found a large **stone circle** (N 92 07) called, like a similar site a few miles away, the **Piper's Stones**. The trees that grow between the stones around the circumference are interesting - ash, thorn and holly - all sacred to the Celts, with the thorn also invariably associated with the Little People in Ireland. Longstone townland, a quarter mile north-west, takes its name from the **Long Stone**, a fallen 13′ 6″ **pillarstone** of granite (N 92 08).

Ballymore, County Westmeath

(Sheet 12) There are two local hills of considerable interest to megalith hunters. The nearest is Bryanmore, about three and a half miles west-south-west of the village which features the remains of a **ring fort** (N 16 48).

The second hill, five miles to the east, is something of a gem. It is the **Hill of Uisneach** (N 29 48), which is believed to mark the *Umbilicus Hiberniae*, or precise centre of Ireland. It was venerated as sacred in ancient times and was the site of a Fire Cult which celebrated the great Bealtaine (Beltane or May Day) Festival still honoured by modern witchcraft. (See boxed reference on page 49.)

The site has a large number of prehistoric remains, not all of them marked on the Ordnance Survey, so a freestyle exploration is recommended. Look out for the **Cat Stone** at the centre of a 60-feet wide **earthen ring** too low to be considered a fort. Experts consider the stone a **glacial erratic**, but its position suggests it may have been deliberately sited, unless the earthwork was specifically built around it. The Cat Stone is located to the north of the Ballymore-Mullingar road on the south-west slope of the hill.

On the summit, you will find what is left of **St Patrick's Bed**, a rectangular **stone platform** which has suffered damage in modern times.

B

Beltane

Beltane or Bealtaine is May 1, a terminal date in the ancient Celtic calendar deriving its name from Beltene, the god of life and death. The eve of Beltane was a time of celebration in pre-Christian Ireland. A bush was decorated with marsh marigolds and placed outside the door to warn off the fairy folk and bonfires were lit to purify the cattle which were driven through them.

Traditionally, the High King lit the first bonfire, but St Patrick beat him to it on the first May Eve following his arrival. A Druid prophet scented danger in the smoke and insisted that if the fire was not extinguished at once, it would burn forever. The warning was ignored, several of the King's Court converted to Christianity and the light of that great religion has burned fiercely in the country ever since.

In Togherstown there is a **ring fort**, while another **ring fort** (N 32 47) stands on the south-east of the hill in Rathnew. This latter fort was the subject of excavations in the middle and late 1920s when it was found partially to cover an even older **ritual circle**.

Ballymote, County Sligo

(Sheet 7) The Town of the Moat takes its name from a 13th-century Anglo-Norman motte, the remains of which can still be seen a mile and a quarter west of the town. Megalith hunters will have to travel a little further, however. The most interesting of the ancient sites are four miles south-east on Keshcorran Mountain.

A climb to the top will be rewarded by sight of a great **cairn** and a large **ring fort** (G 71 12). Less hardy visitors might find it easier to explore the numerous small caves on the west face which, archaeologists assure us, were once used as human habitations. Also

Cormac

Cormac MacArt was a 3rd-century High King of Ireland who owned a magical cup said to break in three if lies were told in its presence, but miraculously restored itself if it heard three truths.

Perhaps aided by the cup, Cormac became known as an exceptional judge and was instrumental in formulating Ireland's ancient Brehon Laws.

One of his greatest accomplishments was the rebuilding of the forts at Tara, the coronation site of the High Kings, but he lost an eye in battle and consequently had to abdicate since it was an immutable law that the Irish High King must be whole of body.

On his deathbed, Cormac left instructions that he be buried at Ros na Riogh, but the Druid priests ignored his wish and planned to have him interred at Brugh na Boinne instead. As the corpse was being ferried across the River Boyne, the waters rose up in outrage and carried Cormac to Ros na Riogh where he was finally buried.

worth a visit is **Cormac's Well**, about a mile away in Cross, where the great Irish hero left the imprint of his head on a stone while being born.

Ballyragget, County Kilkenny

(Sheet 18) This village was named for its Norman landowners in the 13th century, but three miles south-south-west in Rathbeaghan is an unusual construction sometimes classified as a **ring fort**, sometimes as a **henge** (S 43 67).

Ballyshannon, County Donegal

(Sheet 3) The market town lies at the head of the Erne estuary and the falls at the river mouth are named after one of the old gods of Eireann, Aed Rúad.

Two miles north-north-east in the townland of

Twomilestone is the **Twomile Stone** itself (G 89 64), a **standing stone** set on a limestone ridge. The megalith is more than eight feet high and five feet wide. It is surrounded by the irregular field banks, mounds and low, protruding stones which mark an early habitation site. The area includes the remains of several earth and stone huts which were excavated to produce worked flint and other implements. There are the remains of two **cashels** in the area, which seems to have been inhabited from late prehistoric times right up to the Middle Ages.

Just over three miles north-west, you can orient yourself at the ruins of Kilbarron Castle, then go south-east - i.e. back the way you came - for the better part of a mile to find the **Giant's Grave** a **wedge tomb** (G 84 64).

In Coolbeg, half a mile south-south-west of Belalt Strand (itself five miles north of Ballyshannon) you will find the remnants of a **court tomb** (G 87 68).

Ballyvaghan, County Clare

(Sheet 14) Ballyvaghan is a port village on the southern shore of Galway Bay and one of the favourite centres for exploring the Burren, a district not simply unique in Ireland, but in the whole of Western Europe. (See boxed reference on page 66.)

The Burren contains rock structures not found elsewhere, plants which grow nowhere else in Ireland and an unusually rich assortment of megalithic remains.

Make your first call at the spectacular **Aillwee Cave** (M 23 05), two miles south of the village. Once the home of bears and, it is believed, the centre of a prehistoric bear cult, the galleries and caverns have been turned into a major tourist attraction - and one well worth visiting. Lighting and walkways have been installed, with guided tours run on a year-round basis

for a small admission charge. If the tour leaves you hungry as well as breathless, there is a restaurant in the entrance building.

If you take the Corrofin Road out of Ballyvaghan and travel two and a half miles south to Ballyallaban, you will find to the west of the road **Cahermore ring fort** (M 21 05) a stone construction with Medieval remains.

On the south-west slope of Ballyallaban Hill, about a mile and a half south-east of Cahermore is a **wedge tomb** (M 23 04). You will find three more **wedge tombs** half a mile to the south in Gleninsheen (M 23 03).

Two miles south of the Gleninsheen tombs, you will find one of the most photographed **dolmens** in the country, **Poulnabrone portal tomb** (M 23 01). The structure lies to the east of the road and is clearly visible from it. (In summer, just look out for the long line of visitors' cars.) Climb the stile and cross a stretch of rocky ground to stand by the dolmen itself. Recent (1986) excavations produced human remains, pottery and artefacts which have helped date the site to about 2,500 BC. The dolmen stands on the Burren's limestone pavement at the centre of a low, circular **cairn** about 30 feet in diameter. The north-facing entrance is just over six feet high, topped by a thin 12 x 7 feet capstone. Just under a mile south of Poulnabrone dolmen is a stone **ring fort** (R 23 99).

From Caherconnell Crossroads, travel a mile south-south-west to Poulawack to find an eight-foot high, 70-feet diameter **cairn** (R 23 98) which yielded burial remains when it was excavated in the 1930s. Harvard archaeologists discovered a dry wall ring encompassing six **cists** within the cairn. Fourteen people had been buried there, with a further two cremations, probably in early Bronze Age times. Along with the bodies were potsherds, an oyster shell,

a bone scraper and a boar's tusk. A mile and a quarter south-south-east, you can orient yourself at St Cronan's, an early monastic site marked by the ruins of a 15th/16th-century church. Just under two miles south-south-east of the ruin, in the townland of Deerpark, you will find a **wedge tomb** (R 24 94).

Three and a half miles south-west of Ballyvaghan is Derrynavahagh **wedge tomb** (M 17 05) generally held to be among the finest examples of megalithic architecture in the Burren.

Take the N67 road to Lisdoonvarna from Ballyvaghan. Four miles out you will find Corkscrew Hill, two miles south of which you will see Cahermacnaghten **ring fort** (M 19 00), an ancient structure with Medieval castellations. This fort was occupied right up to the end of the 17th century and was at one time a Gaelic law school.

Baltinglass, County Wicklow

(Sheet 16) Baltinglass, or *Bealach Conglais*, is named for the ancient highway known as the road, or pass, of Cuglas, a legendary hero. It was founded around 1148 with the establishment of the Cistercian Abbey of Vallis Salutis, whose ruins can still be visited in the town. The surrounding area is particularly rich in megalithic sites.

Closest to the town, but not, unfortunately, accessible by road, are the remains of a **chambered cairn** (S 88 89) near the summit of Baltinglass Hill, overlooking the town to the east-north-east. Six of the stones show spiral and other motifs. In the same general area is the Rathcoran **hill fort**, guarding the pass from a height of more than 1,200 feet.

Some three and a half miles east of Baltinglass are the **Gates of Glory** (S 92 88), two **orthostats** and sill in the yard of the ruined Kilranelagh Church, one of the earliest Christian sites in the district. To find the

site, head east-south-east for Talbotstown Upper, then north for a mile and a quarter for Colvinstown Upper. If you had died here when the church was still standing, your coffin would have been carried through the Gates to ensure your entry into heaven – an intriguing survival of what was undoubtedly a much earlier pre-Christian practice.

If you do decide to see the Gates of Glory, it's a short (one and a half mile) step east to Boleycarrigeen where you will find an **ogham stone** in the rampart of Crossoona **rath** (S 94 88) and, quite close by, the **Griddle Stones**, an embanked **stone circle** of 11 complete stones and the remains of a twelfth.

Just under six miles north-east of the town is Castleruddery **Stone Circle** (S 91 94) at Castleruddery Lower. Take the Dublin Road out of Baltinglass and start looking for the signpost after about four miles. Turn right, heading for the Wicklow Mountains, and climb a steep, narrow, but reasonably well-surfaced road to find the circle in a field on your right. The circle itself is enclosed by a shallow earthen bank with two white quartz portal stones flanking the entrance. The site is still very atmospheric, particularly by moonlight, and there are some interesting alignments with gaps on the mountain horizon.

A little over ten miles from Baltinglass by the side of the Dublin Road at Athgreany are the **Piper's Stones** (N 93 03), forming one of the most delightful **stone circles** in the country. The site is signposted, although at time of writing the pointer has been broken so that only the words 'PIP STO' remain. While just a short distance away on a hilltop (the stones are actually visible from the road a little way on from the signpost) it is advisable to bring boots, especially in winter, when the ground underfoot can get marshy and a little stream runs parallel to the road. Climb the gate on the roadside, follow the path, then turn right in the field and struggle up the hill until the stones suddenly appear. The site is well worth the effort.

As with virtually all 'Piper's Stones' throughout the British Isles, this ring has attracted the legend that a group of merrymakers were dancing to a piper's tune on the Sabbath when God turned them to stone for desecrating the holy day. The 14 granite circle stones were the dancers, while a massive **outlier** 40 yards north-east is said to have been the piper. While the theme of ossification as punishment recurs quite often in Gaelic folklore, a more pertinent clue to the nature of the site might be contained in the district name, Athgreany, which translates as 'Field of the Sun', suggesting ceremonial usage.

A very old thorn tree, invariably associated with the fairy folk in Ireland, grows, although fallen, on the circumference of the circle, with another a short way off. P. A. O'Síocháin, in his fascinating book *Ireland: A Journey into Lost Time*, says there is a much larger, but completely ruined, stone circle in the field at the bottom of the hill with the remains of other megalithic structures. It is certainly true that there are a great many stones of varying sizes to be seen in this field, but it is almost impossible to determine whether or not these are natural placings.

Bandon, County Cork

(Sheet 25) Five miles north-east of the town at Clashanimud, is a **hill fort**, known as **Cashel Fort** (W 52 61).

Bantry, County Cork

(Sheet 24) If you can take your eyes off the scenic delights provided by Bantry Bay, travel five miles north-east to Kealkill where you will find a **stone**

circle, two **pillarstones** and a **cairn** (V 05 55). The circle is one of the smallest in the country, only eight feet in diameter and constructed of five stones standing only three to four feet high. Archaeologists who excavated the site in 1938 discovered remains of a timber structure which may have been used in conjunction with the circle for astronomical sightings. The taller of the two stones was once taller still. Its original height was around 20 feet, but it fell, broke and the 12-foot stump was re-erected. The remains of the cairn lie just a few feet south of the pillarstones. Archaeologists believe it to be a rare example of a **ring cairn** similar to those found in Aberdeenshire in Scotland. Such cairns are usually associated with stone circles. This one had another circle of sorts inside it, originally 18 stones, but not, curiously enough, concentric with the cairn.

Seven miles south-west of Bantry on the L56, you will reach Dunbeacon. Take the by-road over Mount Corin. Where it crosses the shoulder of the mountain, you will find a quarter mile to the west a fine **stone circle** surrounding a central **monolith** (V 92 38). On the other side of the road (i.e. east) in the townland of Coolcoulaghta, you can see in a field two **pillarstones**, re-erected in modern times.

From Bantry through Carrigboy and Durrus on the road to the Sheep's Head Peninsula you will find 12 miles south-west an ancient well known as Dromnea Well. Some 400 yards east-south-east are **pillarstones** (V 84 37), while four and a half miles south-west, in the townland of Caherurlagh, is Ballyroon **Hole Stone** (V 76 35).

Bellanagare, County Roscommon

(Sheet 12) Half a mile east-south-east of the village is a small **ring fort** (M 75 87). An interesting **ogham stone** is set on the rampart.

Belmullet, County Mayo

(Sheet 6) Four and a half miles west-north-west of the port, right in the sand dunes is a **pillarstone** within a circular enclosure (F 63 35).

Five and a half miles north-west of the town you will find the remains of **Doonamo**, a **cliff fort** (F 64 37). You can still see (but only just) signs of its original megalithic fortifications.

If you can manage a 14-mile trip to the south-west tip of the Mullet, there are a great many early Christian remains, but to the north of the harbour you will find two concentric **stone circles** surrounding a **pillarstone** (F 64 19).

Belturbet, County Cavan

(Sheet 8) There is an unusual historic/prehistoric site a mile and a half east in Magherintemple where you will find a hilltop graveyard, which once sported a Medieval Church. The church was sited, as Christian churches often were, on a pagan religious site - in this case a large, oval **earthwork** (H 39 17) which you can still see.

Birr, County Offaly,

(Sheet 15) As one of the old garrison towns, Birr has a great deal of interesting local history, but little enough for the megalith hunter. If, however, you travel six miles south-east to the Saighir Cíaráin monastic site, you may, according to the assurances of some scholars, be standing on the sacred site of a pre-Christian **fire temple** (N 13 02).

Blacklion, County Cavan

(Sheet 7) Only a mile and a half west of the village on a promontory of Upper Lough Macnean's southern shore you will find **St Brigid's Stone** and two other sandstone boulders (H 05 38). All three have rounded

or ovoid quartzite **cursing stones** in smooth, cup-like depressions on their upper surfaces. You can curse your relatives, boss, traffic warden, or Income Tax inspector by turning these stones in their sockets. But beware, since an unjust curse rebounds on your own head.

(Rumour has it that there was once a **pillarstone** beside St Brigid's Stone. It was called the **Crom Cruaich** in honour of an elder god of ancient Ireland. (See boxed reference below.) If the stone was ever there, it is not there now: folklorists say it was moved near Belcoo, County Fermanagh, in Northern Ireland where it can still be seen.)

Two miles south of the village is a notable group of **megaliths** (H 08 35) in barren mountain limestone

Crom Cruaich

The fifth ruler of Ireland, High King Tighernmas, is remembered for two things. The first was that he established a social colour coding which allowed slaves to wear only one colour, while the upper classes, such as poets, could wear as many as six. The second was his introduction of the worship of the Crom Cruaich.

The Crom Cruaich, or Bloody Crescent, was a serpent god, which provided the inspiration for one of Bram Stoker's less well-known horror novels, *The Lair of the White Worm*. Its image was erected on Magh Shleacht, the Plain of Destruction, in County Cavan, and the first born of the country were sacrificed to it.

King Tighernmas actually dropped dead while engaged in an act of worship at the bloody altar. Sacrifice to the Crom Cruaich continued to be practised until St Patrick's Christianity broke the power of this dark religion - commemorated to this day in the legend of Patrick banishing the snakes from Ireland.

country similar to the **Burren** in Clare. (See boxed reference on page 66.) The **cairns** extend into County Fermanagh (i.e. you have to cross the Border into Northern Ireland) but also run northwards towards Lough Macnean. The group includes the **Giant's Grave**, a **wedge tomb**, the kerb of which is 36 feet long. The main chamber is 17 feet long, narrowing from four feet to three feet in width and divided by cross slabs from two further chambers. The westernmost of the five capstones has **ring** and **cup marks**.

Four miles south-south-west of the village, in Moneygashel, are the remains of three quite well preserved stone **ring forts** (H 05 34), about half a mile north of the school. The largest of these has an internal diameter of about 80 feet. To the south, you can inspect the unusual feature of external stone stairs which run up the wall. The entrance to this fort is to the east and inside you will find two more staircases. In another fort of the group 500 yards south-west, you will find a stone beehive-shaped structure about 12 feet in diameter. This is of comparatively modern origin and functioned as a sweathouse.

Blarney, County Cork

(Sheet 25) The best-known 'megalith' in this wool-manufacturing village five miles north-west of Cork City is the world-famous 'Blarney Stone', just below the battlements of the 15th-century Blarney Castle. Both the castle and its 18th-century demesne are open to visitors for a small fee, but the ballyhoo which surrounds the practice of kissing the Blarney Stone (in order to develop the gift of the gab) has obscured the fact that the demesne also houses two of the most interesting great stone monuments in the country.

Blarney Stone

Cleena (or Cliodhna) was a beautiful maiden of the Tuatha Dé Danaan (see boxed reference on page 116) who had the misfortune to fall in love with a mortal man, the handsome Keevan of the Curling Locks. Despite Keevan's unfortunate reputation - he was drummed out of the Fianna warrior brotherhood (see boxed reference on page 44) for immorality - they ran off together, but Cleena was swept home to her own country by a miraculous wave, commemorated to this day in the Cork placename Tonn Cliodhna, the Wave of Cleena. As daughter of Chief Druid Gebann, Cleena became a Fairy Queen of Munster.

In this capacity, she was called on by Cormac MacCarthy, the 15th-century builder of Blarney Castle, for help in a lawsuit. Cleena told him to kiss the first stone he saw in the morning. Cormac did so and argued his case with such dazzling rhetoric that he won the suit.

Concerned that the stone's powers would turn Ireland into a nation of glib liars, Cormac hid it away in a wall of his castle where it is regularly kissed to this day, mainly by American tourists.

In the demesne, follow signs to the 'Druid's Stones' or 'Rock Close'. You will eventually reach a fine example of a **dolmen** immediately beside the path (W 61 75). Just beyond the dolmen on higher ground is a **stone circle** enclosed in a wooded dell, but this is far more recent - despite appearances, it was created as part of some eccentric landscape gardening, in the 17th century.

Blessington, County Wicklow

(Sheet 16) Although surrounded by some magnificent lake scenery, the Blessington area is sparse in megalithic remains. Six miles east-north-east, however, on the summit of Seefin Mountain, is a round **cairn** (O 08 17). This covers an interesting **passage grave** with a number of chambers and subchambers and two patterned uprights.

B

Bohonagh, County Cork

(Sheet 24) On a hilltop within a mile of the coast you will find a delightful **stone circle** (W 30 36) which features matched portal stones to the east more than seven feet tall - probably the highest matched pair in any Irish circle. The site was excavated in 1959, during which three of the original 13 stones were re-erected, leaving nine now standing in a 30-foot ring. The circle is aligned to the summer equinox sunset and a short distance east you will find a **boulder burial** with a cup marked capstone. The site as a whole is probably Bronze Age.

Cabinteely, County Dublin

(Sheet 16) Brenanstown **portal tomb** (O 22 24), signed as a national monument, lies only a mile south-west of this Dublin suburb in the valley of Glen Druid beside a stream. It is an impressive dolmen with a granite capstone varying in width from three to five feet and weighing an estimated 40 tons. There are two deep gutters on top of the capstone, one of which has ducts leading to the corners – a feature found on some of the Newgrange capstones.

Caherdaniel, County Kerry

(Sheet 24) On the slopes of Mount Tullig, about half a mile to the west of the village on the Kenmare-Waterville road is a stone **ring fort** in excellent repair (V 54 59).

A mile and a half south-west, on the shore, is an **ogham stone** (V 53 57).

Three miles north-east-north of the Sneem-Parknasilla road, is **Staigue Fort** (V 61 63), one of the most impressive **ring forts** you are likely to see. The ramparts of this stone fort are 13 feet thick, rising to a height of 18 feet and contain two small chambers. The whole structure is in a remarkable state of preservation, a tribute to the ancient masons who built the walls entirely without mortar. The entrance is to the south, a six-feet high passage roofed with enormous lintels. From inside, you can gain access to the ramparts by means of several flights of steps.

Three and a half miles west, an interesting **wedge tomb** lies near the top of Coumakista Pass (V 50 60).

Callan, County Kilkenny

(Sheet 18) There are a great many historical sites of interest within striking distance of this market town, but little for the megalith hunter. If, however, you travel six miles north-north-west to Kilmanagh to see where St Nadal founded an early Christian monastery, you might travel just over half a mile south-west from there to see the **Potter's Ring Fort – Pottlerath** or **Rath an Photaire** (S 38 51).

Camp, County Kerry

(Sheet 20) This small village, 10 miles south-west of Tralee, lies close to some extraordinarily interesting historic and prehistoric megalithic sites.

Only about 400 yards south-east of the village on the slopes of Caherconree Mountain is an **ogham stone** (Q 69 08) with the addendum of a short forged inscription.

Travel two miles west-south-west to Foilatrisnig where you will find close together three **pillarstones** and a **ring fort** (Q 67 08). The stones are known locally as the **Stones of the Lunatics** (indeed the area is sometimes called the **Valley of the Lunatics**) since the insane were sometimes taken to them in bygone days in the hope of a magical cure.

Two miles south-south-west in the townland of Maumnahaltora are two **chamber tombs** (Q 68 06).

Two and a half miles south-east of the village, you can approach Caherconree by way of the Finglas Valley and thus, if you have the energy for an extremely strenuous climb, see the remains of a great

Cú-Raoi mac Dáire

The name of the Finglas Valley (which means valley of the white stream) derives from the treachery of the wife of Ireland's great mythic hero Cú-Raoi mac Dáire. She poured milk into the stream to signal to her husband's enemies that Cú-Raoi was in residence at his stronghold. Alerted by the warning, they climbed the mountain stealthily, mounted a surprise attack and murdered him.

promontory fort (Q 72 06) known as **Cathair Chon-Raoi** and associated with the ancient warrior Cú-Raoi mac Dáire.

Campile, County Wexford

(Sheet 23) West-north-west of this village on the New Ross–Ramsgrange road is Great Island, a district which used to be an island. If you travel about three miles from Campile to the northern end of the 'island' you will find Kilmokea and the remains of an enormous near-circular **earthwork**. In its original form it was close on a thousand feet in diameter with two banks of earth and stones separated by a ditch. Today, only segments remain.

Carlingford, County Louth

(Sheet 9) Only about a mile south-south-west of this Carlingford Lough resort, you will reach the townland of Commons where, on the slopes of Slieve Foye, you will find two **court tombs** (J 18 10).

Some six to seven miles south-west of the town at Rockmarshall House, National Monument signs will point you to a third **court tomb** (J 12 08) with an interesting long gallery.

Carlow, County Carlow

(Sheet 19) This bustling cathedral town and county capital boasts one of the most remarkable megalithic monuments in the country. Take the Hacketstown Road out of Carlow and travel approximately two miles east to Kernanstown, where the signpost will point you to **Browne's Hill dolmen** (S 75 76).

The **portal tomb** itself is deceptive. It looks almost insignificant from the road and for most of a lengthy pedestrian approach. (There is ample off-road parking if you drive there, incidentally.) But the dolmen is breathtaking when you actually reach it, since it has the largest capstone of any megalithic monument in Ireland, estimated to weigh in excess of 100 tons. One expert has claimed it to be the largest stone of its type in Europe. It measures about 20 feet square and is five feet thick. The cap rests on three six-feet tall uprights and two prostrate stones.

Four miles south-south-east of Carlow is the site of a Neolithic **cist burial** (S 74 70). Although there is little enough to see now, ploughing across the low, 28-yard diameter mound brought to light a large megalithic cist made from seven granite blocks and two capstones. It contained the bones of a dismembered body, a polished stone axe and several potsherds.

Carran, County Clare

(Sheet 14) The village is located in good megalith-hunting country, with the astonishing Burren district sweeping to the west. (See boxed reference on page 66.)

For an excellent day out, travel a mile south to Castletown, which is a good starting point for your hunt. A mile south-south-west in Tullycommon, you would be hard put to miss the stone **ring fort** (R 28 96) of Cashlaungarr, which dominates a rocky

The Burren

The name Burren translates as a 'rocky place', an accurate enough interpretation which nevertheless does small justice to this unique limestone sweep of County Clare. The limestone was laid down as marine sediment in carboniferous times, compressed into layered rock by its own weight. Erosion produced the hills and valleys evident today while Ice Age glaciers deposited rock, gravel and clay.

Today the Burren is known for fauna found nowhere else in Europe and for its ancient megaliths. Towards the end of the Stone Age, early farmers were drawn to the district by the dry and lightly wooded highlands. They embarked on clearance, moved in their herds and, over the centuries, aided the continuing process of erosion by overgrazing. The result is the stark landscape now evident.

The Burren is one of the best-known and richest concentrations of ancient sites in Ireland. The last official megalithic survey pinpointed a total of 66 tombs, mainly wedge tombs. There are close on 500 ring forts. Both forts and burials have been preserved by a strong local tradition associating them with the Fairy Folk best left alone.

In this Guide, several Burren monuments are listed under their nearest population centres, such as Lisdoonvarna and Kilfenora. But these listings cannot - and do not - cover more than a small fraction of the sites worth visiting.

To enjoy the megalithic treasures of the Burren fully, buy a copy of T.D. Robinson's Burren map at the Burren Display Centre in Kilfenora, lace up your hiking boots and spend as many days or weeks as you have to spare in exploration.

pinnacle by the roadside at Cahercommaun. This is the largest and strongest structure of its kind in the country. Although easy to see it is difficult to reach.

Archaeological work in 1934 unearthed stone axes as well as later iron tools, showing a lengthy continuity of occupation. In a **souterrain** on the western side, a human skull and silver brooch (dated at around AD 800) were discovered. The sheer size of the fort is almost overwhelming. Some of the inner ring walling reaches a thickness of 28 feet and at one point rises to a height of 14 feet. There are the remnants of about a dozen **stone buildings** within the fortifications. Check out the largest of these for a 20-feet long **souterrain**.

A mile and a half due east of Castletown, in Cappaghkennedy, is a worthwhile **wedge tomb** (R 30 97). It is one of the best preserved in the Burren and is situated on a ridge at a height of about 750 feet. Although it has two capstones now, experts believe these may have originally formed a single slab. The tomb was used to house a family in the 19th century.

Carrigart, County Donegal

(Sheet 1) Three miles north of the village, a narrow path leads to Mevagh Old Church on Mulroy Bay. South-west of the site is a hill on which you will find a series of interesting **rock scribings** (C 12 39).

Castletown Bearhaven, County Cork

(Sheet 24) Just under five miles north-north-west of the port, overlooking Ballycovane Bay, is a large **ogham stone** (V 65 53).

Castletownsend, County Cork

(Sheet 24) In Knockdrum, just three quarters of a mile north-west of the village, you will find a fine stone **ring fort** (W 17 31) restored by the National Monuments Commission. Known, appropriately enough, as The Fort, it surrounds the remnants of a **clochán** and three **souterrains**.

Perhaps even more interesting are the **cup marks** on the stone outside - almost forty in all. Ring and cup marks are a feature of many megaliths in Britain and have been found as megalithic culture traces as far afield as Tibet, but are less common in Ireland. This boulder probably dates to the early Bronze Age and may have no real connection with the fort.

A few hundred yards north-north-west of the site is an alignment of **pillarstones**, known as the **Three Fingers**. These slim stones, some 14 feet high, are set in joints in the exposed bedrock. At present they form a simple linear alignment, but the stump of a fourth pillar is nearby, breaking the neat alignment and suggesting that what we have here is the last remnants of a more complex megalithic monument.

Cavan, County Cavan

(Sheet 8) About three and a quarter miles north-east of the town high on a barren hillside at Shantemon, you will find **Finn MacCool's Fingers** (H 46 07), an alignment of **standing stones**, four of them still upright. (See boxed reference on page 90.)

Five miles south-south-east of the town is **Worm Ditch** (N 44 97), an ancient **earthwork** running along the western and southern slopes of Ardkill Mountain in the townlands of Ardkill More and Largan. At one time, archaeologists thought the Ditch might be connected with Black Pig's Dyke, which lies 14 miles north-north-east (see boxed reference on page 101) but the consensus now is that it is a large, but purely local fortification.

Clear Island, County Cork

(Sheet 24) Your best bet to reach Clear Island is by boat from Baltimore. About a mile south-south-east of North Harbour (also known as Traigh Chiarain) is a hill overlooking South Harbour where you will find an **alignment of stones** and a **pillarstone** (V 96 20). There was once a slab with interesting **spiroform decorations**, but this has been taken to Cork City Museum.

Cliffoney, County Sligo

(Sheet 7) The village itself lies on the Bundoran–Sligo road. There are two interesting megalithic sites in the locality. The nearest is about a mile north-east, where you will find the spectacular Creevykeel **court tomb** (G 72 54) to the east of the Bundoran road behind a cottage. The site comprises a **cairn**, an entrance passage, a court and a double chamber gallery. Excavations in 1935 unearthed pottery, stone axes and other artefacts and, most important of all, four cremation burials. Restoration work was carried out shortly afterwards. The cairn is wedge shaped, tapering towards the west with a court which exceeds 50 feet in length. To the west of the court, you will find the entrance to the long gallery where most of the artefacts and the cremations were found. The **orthostats** flanking the gallery entrance are six feet high. There is a segment of ruined wall in the court which is of far more recent origin than the remainder of the tomb. It seems a family (or family business!) moved into the tomb in early Christian times. The wall is all that remains of a drying kiln.

The second site is two and a half miles north of Cliffoney, at Bunduff Strand where you will find a **court tomb** (G 71 57) in good condition.

Clonakilty, County Cork

(Sheet 25) A mile and a half north of the market town at Templebryan, is the site of an ancient church which includes a tall **pillarstone** (W 48 43) with an **ogham** inscription just discernible. There is a **bullaun** nearby, known locally as the **Wart Well**, presumably

because it is reputed to cure this sort of affliction. A couple of fields away to the south-east, you will find the remains of a roadside **stone circle**. The circle is approximately 30 feet in diameter and surrounds a low **pillarstone** of white quartz. Five stones out of an original eight remain.

A similar distance east-south-east there is a spectacularly-sited **wedge tomb** (W 30 36) at Ahaglaslin. It lies on a ledge below a steep rock face and you would be advised to content yourself with a roadside view of it. It looks like a dolmen with its large, 13 x 18 feet, capstone and is oriented towards the east, but most authorities agree the double walling and typical tapered shape place it in the wedge tomb category.

Clonmacnois, County Offaly

(Sheet 15) Clonmacnois is, of course, one of the foremost early monastic sites in the whole of Ireland with an incredible array of historical monuments and sights of interest. If you can tear yourself away from these long enough to make the three mile trip east, you will find near Clonfinlough Church an impressive **boulder**, called the **Clonfinlough Stone** (N 04 29), with prehistoric **scribings**.

Clonmel, County Tipperary

(Sheets 22, 18) The county town of Tipperary has a great many ecclesiastical sites of interest, but few prehistoric monuments. A trip three miles north-west to Giantsgrave, however, will take you to a **pillarstone** (S 17 26) with two inscribed crosses. The monument is known locally as the **Giant's Broad Stone**.

Cloyne, County Cork

(Sheet 25) Three miles west-south-west of the village

on the shore near Rostellan Castle is a **megalithic chamber** (W 88 67), re-erected in modern times. If you have difficulty finding it, wait until the tide goes out since it actually lies about 30 feet below high water mark. The megalith is approximately six feet high and seven feet long, aligned east-west on a limestone pavement. Archaeologists discovered a **shell midden** to the south-west.

Coachford, County Cork

(Sheet 21) For most visitors, Coachford means angling. For the megalith hunter, a three mile trip south to Roovesmore will be rewarded by sight of a large **ring fort** (W 45 68). There used to be three **ogham stones** in the **souterrain** of the fort, but these now rest in the British Museum.

Three miles north-north-west of Donaghmore village (itself six miles north-north-east of Coachford) the townland of Gowlane North sports a **stone circle** and **entrance passage** (W 47 86).

These monuments are only the start of a particularly rich harvest in the locality. Take the road from Coachford through Peak and drive a little over four miles in total to find the ruined church of St Olann due west of Peak. Look south-east to see the **ogham pillarstone** (W 43 75) crowned by a quartz crystal. Local belief holds that the stone has magical properties and will cure a variety of ailments. Until the early 1830s, there were two capstones, one on top of the other, creating a marvellously phallic monument. The parish priest objected and had the capstones removed, but his parishioners promptly replaced them with the existing cap.

North of the pillarstone is a **boulder** on which the fanciful see the imprint of **St Olann's feet**, while 450 yards north-north-east is a **clochán** covering St Olann's well.

Stand at the well and look south to see another **ogham stone**. It is not on its original site, but was found at a nearby **ring fort** (now sadly obliterated) and set up in the 19th century.

Even this does not exhaust the riches of the district. Orient yourself by going to Sheskinny Cross, which lies two miles north-west of the well. From the cross, travel the westerly road for half a mile to reach a **stone circle** in Oughtihery (W 40 81).

Three quarters of a mile south-west of the cross at Knockrour you will find the ruins of Kill church. Two **pillarstones** (W 40 80) flank the entrance. Examine them carefully to find an **ogham** inscription on one of them.

A mile east of the cross in Rylane is a **stone circle** (W 42 81). If you cross two fields to the east of the circle, you will find a **pillarstone**. A further mile east of the circle in the district of Kilcullen South, there are two **pillarstones** (W 44 81), one with **ogham**, marking an ancient cemetery.

Two miles north of the cross, in Knocknagoun, you will find a **stone circle** (W 40 84). There is a **wedge tomb** a little to the east.

Cobh, County Cork

(Sheet 25) Three miles south of the port on Curraghbinny Hill overlooking Cork Harbour, you will find a 70 feet diameter **cairn** (W 79 62). The site was excavated in 1932 and a clay platform covered in charcoal found at the centre. The cairn itself had originally been built, probably during the Bronze Age, inside a boulder kerb of more than 50 feet in diameter. The shore at the bottom of the hill gave evidence of several **middens**.

Collooney, County Sligo

(Sheet 7) Slieve Daeane lies three miles north-east of

The Cailleach

The name given to the passage tomb on Slieve Daeane is particularly interesting in that *cailleach* links it both with witchcraft and ancient pre-Christian fertility rites.

The term means a hag or a witch, but has an alternative meaning as the last sheaf of corn to be harvested in any given season. This sheaf had magical properties. Part was fed to the cattle, part shaken over the land - both practices meant to ensure fertility.

To this day, country girls avoid tying up the last sheaf since to do so ruins their chances of finding a husband.

the town. South-west of the summit is a **passage tomb** known locally as **Cailleach Bhearra's House** (G 71 29).

Cong, County Mayo

(Sheet 11) The village where *The Quiet Man* was filmed has a marvellous ruined abbey and some interesting caves which tourists are encouraged to visit. Less well publicised are the district's megalithic sites. Only a mile and a quarter north-east is a collection of no less than four **stone circles** (M 16 56) set close together in the neighbouring townlands of Glebe and Tonalecaun.

Take the road east out of the village on the L98A and travel two miles in the direction of Cross to find (north of the road) an interesting **passage tomb** (M 18 55).

Coolaney, County Sligo

(Sheet 7) The **Giant's Grave** (G 57 25), a good example of a **wedge tomb**, lies to the south of the Cappagh road two and a half miles west of the village. Further on, in the adjoining townland of Cabragh, are two more **wedge tombs**.

Cootehill, County Cavan

(Sheet 8) Take the L46 Shercock road out of the town and travel three miles south-east, keeping an eye north, and you will be rewarded with sight of a fine, five-chambered **court tomb** with a dual court about 150 yards north-west of the school (H 64 12). The megalith is known locally as **Cohaw Giant's Grave**.

The Grave is just one among a group of court tombs which overlook the Annalee River. Others in the group include a dual court tomb half a mile north-east in Aghagashlan, a single **court tomb** in Mayo half a mile to the north and another half a mile to the south-west.

The Giant's Grave is an 85-feet long rectangular cairn on a north-south alignment. Excavations in 1949 unearthed a skull and several cremated bones along with a Neolithic pot. The stone pegs at the mouths of the forecourts mark the positions of post holes. Just inside the northern court are two socket holes which once held slim **pillarstones** now broken. There is an **orthostat** to the east of the northern gallery.

Seven and a half miles west-north-west, almost on the border with County Monaghan, is a dual **court tomb** (H 48 16) at Drumavrack. You approach the megalith along a narrow lane. The cairn is more than 100 feet long and the north-west court leads to the entrance of a large, triple-chambered gallery. The entrance is interesting in that it is blocked by a six-feet high slab with a small porthole-type opening at the bottom.

Cork, County Cork

(Sheet 25) There is so much to see and do in Cork City that you may find yourself with little time for megalith hunting - which is possibly just as well since there are few sites in the environs.

About two and a quarter miles north-west of the city (a mile west-south-west of Killeens House) three horseshoe **mounds** mark prehistoric **cooking places** (W 63 73). The results of excavations in 1953 were particularly interesting in that they showed evidence of very long-term usage (from about 1700 BC for several centuries) but only for short periods of time every autumn. This suggests a nomadic people returning again and again to traditional camp sites. Underneath the floor of one of the cooking pits, a gold-plated ring was discovered.

Also within striking distance of Cork are **pillarstones** known as the **Long Stones**.

To find the Long Stones, travel three and a quarter miles north, passing Glennamought Bridge, to reach the ruins of Kilcully Church. Just over two miles north-west, in Ballinvarrig, are the Stones (W 65 79).

Craughwell, County Galway

(Sheet 14) The village, seven miles from Loughrea, has one megalith in its vicinity - a **wedge tomb** just under four miles south-east in Toorclogher (M 55 16).

Crookstown, County Cork

(Sheet 25) Four miles from Crookstown, to the south-east in Garranes, is the Lisnacaheragh **ring fort** (W 47 64). This structure, preserved as a national monument, is particularly interesting since it is held to be the birthplace of St Finnbarr. This would suggest a 6th-century dating, but the fort would obviously be older and possibly much older. Excavation in 1937 produced evidence of glass and metal working, with some imported pottery from Gaul. The whole structure was elaborately fortified - four massive wooden gates defended the entrance, for example - but oddly enough there were no indications of any military occupation.

The Pooka

Pooka, or Phuca, is a term used generically in Ireland to denote spirits or fairies, although the word refers specifically to a particular fairy which usually appears in the shape of a black goat. This pooka had the power to curse human enemies by giving them a humpback.

At Hallowe'en, Irish children don masks and fancy dress to masquerade as the pooka and demand sweets or fruit from householders. After Hallowe'en, the real pooka spoils the blackberries.

Adults celebrate the pooka in an even less restrained fashion at the annual Puck Fair, in honour of a goat, held at Killorglin, County Kerry.

Crossmolina, County Mayo

(Sheet 6) Travel a little less than four miles west and look south of the Bangor-Erris N59 road to find one of the most unusual **long cairns** (G 08 17) in the country. This seems to be a **court tomb**, but one which features both a single and a double court - an unlikely piece of megalithic architecture.

Crusheen, County Clare

(Sheet 14) Another **Giant's Grave** here, no more than half a mile south-west of the village in Caheraphuca - a name suggesting spirits associated with the stone. The monument itself is a **wedge tomb** (R 39 87).

Culdaff, County Donegal

(Sheet 2) An unusual megalith here which may or may not be of prehistoric origin. Called **St Bodan's Boat**, it rests in the Culdaff River and indentations on its surface are believed to have been made by the saint's own fingers when he sailed the stone across from Scotland.

A little over a mile from the village on Mass Hill

in the townland of Glacknadrumman is one of County Donegal's only two **stone circles**. The tragedy of this site is that a land clearance operation in the 19th century resulted in the destruction of many of the stones, which were knocked down and in some cases buried. The original circle probably had about 30 stones and a diameter up to 70 feet. Only a few **orthostats** remain, but these are fine specimens up to six feet tall and well worth a visit.

Daingean, County Offaly

(Sheet 15) North of the village lies the Bog of Allen. About four miles north-north-east, you will reach Croghan Hill on which you will find, among several historic sites, a **chambered cairn** (N 48 33).

Dalkey, County Dublin

(Sheet 16) This prosperous resort suburb is not particularly rich in megalithic remains, although there is a **portal tomb** (known as **Shanganagh Dolmen**) a little less than a mile away to the south-south-west near the Ballybrack-Shankill road (O 26 25).

It may, however, be worthwhile taking a boat trip from Coliemore Harbour to Dalkey Island, which is known to have been inhabited in prehistoric times. On the island are the ruins of an ancient church, fronted by a rock with a ringed cross inscription which is probably early Christian, but may possibly be older since the symbol predates the religion to which it is now central.

Excavations on the island have shown Neolithic and Bronze Age deposits with beneath them two **shell middens** (O 27 26) containing flint tools, domestic animal bones and polished stone axes reliably dated to about 3340 BC.

Dingle, County Kerry

(Sheet 20) The megalithic excitement begins in the town itself. At the head of the Main Street you will find a **boulder** (Q 44 01) which displays cup marks and other prehistoric designs.

There is an Iron Age **promontory fort** and **souterrain** on a V-shaped headland near the town to the south-west of the peninsula carefully left unsigned and unlisted in many of the guides because it is in a dangerous condition. Parts of the cliff have fallen into the sea, taking portions of the fort with them. Inland, there are the remains of a massive drystone wall with a series of **earthworks** adding to the defences. The entrance is a 20-feet long roofed passage with sentry chambers in the walls. This is an impressive fort with many interesting features, but if you do visit, heed the warning notices and take care.

A mile and a quarter west of Dingle, just beyond Milltown village, you will find two fallen **pillarstones** (Q 42 01), one of which features cup marks and other designs. Nearby, to the west, is a ruined **chamber tomb**, while to the north you will find a matched pair of **pillarstones** locally named as the **Gates of Glory** with further **pillarstones** in the neighbouring fields.

Two miles to the east is the **pillarstone** of **Gallán Mór** at Ballineetig (Q 47 01).

Two miles north-north-west there is a terraced **ring fort** with **clocháns** at Ballyheabought (Q 43 04).

Two miles south-east, there are nine **ogham stones** (V 46 99) in the graveyard at Ballintaggart. A mile and a quarter east by the **ring fort** you will find the first **ogham stone** to be discovered in modern times, the **Cloch an tSagairt** (V 48 99).

Two and a half miles west-south-west, there are three **ogham stones** (V 41 99) beside the driveway to the old Burnham estate.

If you travel to Lispole, a village four and a half

miles east of Dingle, visit St Martin's Church to the north-west of the bridge - it is surrounded by an **earthwork** which may predate the building itself (Q 51 01).

Five and a half miles north-north-west in the townland of Ballybrack is a **clochán** (Q 42 09). A mile further on, to the north-north-east, you will find **stone forts** and **clocháns** (Q 43 10) in Ballynavenooragh.

Donaghpatrick, County Meath

(Sheet 13) Donaghpatrick, which lies equidistant from Navan and Kells, was named for the great church St Patrick built on a site that is now part of the graveyard attached to the local Protestant church. A mile and a half south of the church is Teltown, the site of a **prehistoric cemetery** (N 81 73) and a remarkable annual Games Festival in honour of the dead celebrated as late as the 12th-century.

A feature of the festival was the Tailteann Marriage, a convenient ceremony which legally bound the couple for only a year and a day. At the end of that time, those wishing to dissolve the union had only to come to **Rath Dubh**, the **Black Ring Fort** now preserved as a National Monument, stand back to back on a north-south axis and walk away from one another out of the fort.

Donard, County Wicklow

(Sheet 16) There is an **ogham stone** (S 93 97) actually in the village, in the garden of the old Civic Guard Station. (The stone was originally sited three miles south-west, on a farm.)

Travel only half a mile north to Box Bridge, to find a **stone** with nineteen **bullauns** and two prehistoric **mounds** (S 93 98).

Two miles north, the **King's Stone** (N 93 00) rests

in Kilbaylet bearing, according to local legend, the imprint of St Kevin's foot.

For the intrepid, the picturesque Glen of Imaal, part of which is now used as a firing range by the Irish Army, lies to the south-east. There are several megaliths in the Glen preserved as National Monuments, including a **pillarstone** (S 98 95) with an **ogham** inscription (**Knickeen Long Stone**) four miles south-east from Donard a little north-east of the ruins of Leitrim Barracks.

One megalith beside an approach road to the Glen is of modern origin. It was erected to commemorate those killed in an explosion at the nearby barracks after World War Two.

Dowra, County Cavan

(Sheet 7) You can find the prehistoric border of Ulster at this pleasant Shannonside village. **Worm Ditch** (N 44 97), a fragment of the frontier **earthwork**, runs for nearly three miles south and south-west of the village to the head of Lough Allen.

Drogheda, County Louth

(Sheet 13) Take your bearings from Townley Hall four miles west of the town on the northern side of the Boyne river then go a half mile south-west to find a **mound** and **passage grave** (O 02 75) marking what was once a **Neolithic village**.

Two miles south-east of Drogheda is Pilltown House, in the grounds of which is an **ogham stone** (O 13 73).

Dromahaire, County Leitrim

(Sheet 7) Two and a half miles east of the village in Mullaghmore is a **court tomb** (G 84 31).

Dromore West, County Sligo

(Sheet 7) This little village on the Dunneill River is a good centre for megalith hunting. Just over two miles south in Belville, you will find a **court tomb** (G 43 30) near the west bank of the river.

Five miles west-south-west (take the main N59 Ballina road) you will reach Culleens. Travel a mile and a half east-south-east of Culleens close to the Owenykeevan River where you will discover the **Griddles of the Fianna** (pronounced fee-anna - see boxed reference on page 44). When you reach them, in an expanse of peat (G 37 28), you will find the **Great Griddle** which is, in fact, a **court tomb**, while the **Small Griddle** is a **wedge tomb**. Both are in a poor state of preservation.

Whoever named the Griddles may have had a hand in naming the **Giant's Griddle** (G 39 28) five miles south-west in Tawnatruffaun and only a mile and a half distant from the Griddles of the Fianna near where the Fiddengarrode River joins the Easky. This is a **portal tomb** forming part of a modern wall into which several of its cairn stones have been built, one of them with a distinctive cup mark. The Griddle and the remains of a second tomb nearby, are both difficult to find and difficult to reach. Ask directions and bring waterproof boots - you will probably be glad you did.

Drumshambo, County Leitrim

(Sheet 7) Just under six miles north-north-east in the Cleigran More district, you will find a **court tomb** (G 99 20).

Drumsna, County Leitrim

(Sheet 12) There is a fascinating prehistoric structure near this village on the Shannon river. The Shannon itself curves in an enormous loop between Drumsha

D

and Jamestown. Sometime in prehistory, the ancient peoples of Ireland erected a ditch and bank earthwork, half a mile long, to cut the loop. Today, remnants of this **earthwork** remain, known as **The Dun** (M 98 96).

Dublin, County Dublin

(Sheet 16) Dublin City began as a Viking settlement rather than a prehistoric site, but it is easy for megalith hunters accustomed to tramping across fields to overlook the fact that some of Ireland's most glorious prehistoric treasures are housed in the National Museum in Kildare Street. When last I visited, there was a spectacular exhibition of gold craftwork dating from the Bronze and Iron Ages.

Four miles south-west of the city centre at Drimnagh are the last remnants of a **tumulus** (O 10 31) usually classified as a **round barrow**. It was once a prominent landmark, but has now been virtually destroyed by gravel working. It was excavated in 1938 at a time when it measured 72 feet across and stood ten feet high. The mound core was a **cairn** dating back to Neolithic times. On top of this was placed a mound of burnt sods with air flues and a covering of logs to create a cremation site. In Bronze Age times, the mound was enlarged with the addition of a sand and gravel layer and surrounded by a **fosse** 20 feet wide and six feet deep.

Six miles south of Dublin city centre on the northern slope of the Wicklow Mountains at Kilmashogue you will find a multiple **cist cairn** with a **portal tomb** (O 15 24) just half a mile to the south-west. Although excavated, the original cairn, oval in plan, gave up no grave goods or other finds, possibly because it had been so much disturbed by later usage. Three of the later cists, however, contained cremations and food vessels. The portal tomb,

Larch Hill Dolmen (O 14 23), is in a ruinous state, although even the remains are impressive with one orthostat rising to a height of almost ten feet.

On Tibradden Mountain in the same area there is a 40-feet diameter **cairn** which covered what was long believed to be a **passage grave**. The dry-walled chamber is now roofless, but both it and the passage are actually Victorian in origin, built to give access when the cairn was excavated in 1849. Originally, the cairn covered only a cist in which were cremation and urn burials and a food vessel.

There is an impressive **dolmen** (O 22 24) seven miles to the south-east at Brenanstown in the valley of Glen Druid. See under **Cabinteely** for details. Close by at Kiltiernan, in the foothills of the Dublin Mountains, you will find a second **portal tomb** (O 19 22), regrettably in a partly collapsed state. The capstone, which measures 22 x 13 feet, is estimated to be some 40 tons in weight. Excavations in 1956 unearthed a chert arrow-head, hollow scrapers and cord-impressed pottery dating to Neolithic times.

Eight miles south-west of Dublin lies Saggart Hill (O 03 24) which has a number of prehistoric remains, including **cairns**, **chamber tombs** and **ring barrows**. Perhaps the most interesting is the **henge monument** at Lugg, a low **tumulus** surrounded by a **ring bank** and ditch. The site was excavated in 1939 when archaeologists discovered that beneath the present structure was an even earlier site consisting of some 160 timber uprights, three fireplaces and a pit. Later, perhaps in the early Iron Age, circular huts were added, then the present structure. The mound held two cremation burials. Around it was evidence of an avenue of timber (and possibly stone) uprights and trilithons. Pottery fragments gave the Iron Age dating, but this is one of those frustrating sites where structural evidence all points towards a much earlier date.

Eight and a half miles south of the city, high on the south eastern slope of Two Rock Mountain, is a **wedge tomb** (O 17 22). This was a much more spectacular site in its day than it is now, since much of the main gallery was pillaged by granite workers in search of raw material. The site was excavated towards the end of the Second World War (or Emergency, as it was called in Ireland) when archaeologists discovered an interesting, perforated, polished stone hammer, flints, pottery and a cup-marked stone block.

Dundalk, County Louth

(Sheet 9) The county town of Louth is an excellent centre for megalith hunting if you take the N1 Newry road north. Between four and five miles on, to the west of the road, are two exceptionally interesting **cairns** (J 07 13). In one is a **portal tomb** now missing its roof slab. In the other are no less than four **chamber tombs**.

About a mile and three quarters south of the latter site in Proleek you will find the grave of an aggressive Scots giant, called **Para Bui Mor Mhac Seoidin** - in actuality a ruined wedge-shaped **gallery tomb** (J 08 11). Nearby is the **Giant's Load**, an impressive tripod **portal tomb** standing 12 feet high. The 'load' carried by this dolmen, the rounded capstone, is estimated to weigh 30 tons or more. It was brought all of a piece from the nearby mountains by a giant named Parrah Boug McShagean, reputedly buried nearby, possibly beneath the dolmen itself. Those of you in search of a wife or husband would be advised to toss a small pebble onto the capstone. If it rolls off, you are out of luck, but if it manages to stay on the rounded surface, you will be married within the year.

Dunfanaghy, County Donegal

(Sheet 1) **Dermot and Grania's Bed**, a **court tomb** in ruinous condition, lies two and a half miles north-north-west of the resort in Claggan (C 00 39).

Dungarvan, County Waterford

(Sheet 22) Travel six miles north-east to Ballykeroge

Diarmaid and Grainne

As the hero of one of ancient Ireland's best-known love stories, Diarmaid (or Dermot) is more properly known as Diarmaid Ua Duibhne, or Diarmaid of the Love Spot. The blemish appeared when a beautiful woman placed a mole in the centre of his forehead.

Diarmaid fell in love with King Cormac MacArt's daughter Grainne (Grania) and eloped with her despite the fact she had been promised to the giant hero Finn MacCool. (See boxed reference on page 90.) The fleeing lovers were pursued by Finn and his warriors, but managed to elude them with the help of Angus Og, the god of love.

The relationship between Diarmaid and Grainne was belatedly consummated after Grainne stepped in a puddle. The water splashed the insides of her thighs and she remarked dryly, 'You are brave in battle, Diarmaid, but I find the water more daring than you.'

The internationally-known story of Tristan and Isolde is based on the Diarmaid and Grainne legend, but the ending of the original is peculiar to Ireland.

Diarmaid had an illegitimate half brother, an individual who became known as the Boar of Ben Bulben, sired on his mother by Roc, a steward to Angus Og. Diarmaid's own father Donn slew the child in a rage, but Roc changed the body into a boar and released the animal with the prophecy that it would eventually kill Diarmaid - which, in the fullness of time, it did.

D

and look for a ruined castle. Nearby is a **boulder** locally referred to as **Cloch Labhrais** (X 32 97). If you are prepared to wait patiently, it may talk to you - this being its legendary power.

A little over six miles to the north-west are limestone **caves** (X 18 94) in Kilgreany, Ballynamintra and Carrigmurish, in one of which were found prehistoric remains which included **human skeletons**.

If you are prepared to travel a little further, you will find near the coast in Ballynamona Lower about four miles south of Ringville (itself about three miles south-south-east of Dungarvan) a **court tomb** usually referred to as **Cailleach Bhearra's House** (X 28 82).

For an odd collection of **ogham stones**, you need to travel north-west three miles to Ballymacmague Cross, drive on the T75 a further seven miles north, then turn off at the sign to Knockboy which is about a mile further on. You are looking for the ruins of the 15th-century St Seskinan's Church (S 21 05), which enclose one such stone and have four more built into the walls.

Dunlavin, County Wicklow

(Sheet 16) A fine centre for the aspiring megalith hunter, Dunlavin has a number of exceptionally interesting sites within easy reach.

Just two miles south, for example, you will find the **ring fort** (S 87 98) of Tornant Moat. Nearby, to the south-east, is what remains of a **tumulus** which yielded a scribed stone now in the National Museum. A little further on, to the east, lie the remains of a **stone circle.**

The same distance north-east takes you to another set of **Piper's Stones** - in this instance simply two granite **boulders** (in neighbouring fields). One of them is inscribed with a cross (N 89 03).

A little more than two miles west, you will reach Brewel Hill, having crossed the border into County Kildare. On the summit are more of the ubiquitous **Piper's Stones** (N 83 01) in the form of three large **boulders** and the **Piper's Chair**, an enormous lump of white quartz.

Three miles east-north-east is a granite **pillarstone** at which marriages used to be celebrated (N 91 02).

Finally, three miles south-west, again in County Kildare, you will have reached Colbinstown and an ancient cemetery featuring no less than nine **pillarstones** and three **ogham stones**, two of which are now broken (S 83 98).

Legend tells that when the King of Munster died, there was a bitter dispute about where he should be buried. To solve it the corpse was put on an ox cart and the beasts left to wander where they liked. As they reached Killeen Cormac, a hound leaped onto a stone in the local graveyard and left an imprint of its paw. The incident was taken as an omen and the king buried. Two of the nine **pillarstones** mark his grave. You will recognise which two by the pawprint on one of them.

Dunmore East, County Waterford

(Sheet 23) Knockadirragh, a commanding hill, lies just over two miles north of Dunmore East. Go to the southern end and climb almost to the summit to find a round **cairn** with its own **passage tomb** (S 67 04). There were three Bronze Age urn burials here, according to archaeologists, but there is a clear suggestion that the original purpose of the monument was not a grave site in that the earliest (Neolithic) deposits were magical and utilitarian in nature.

Dunquin, County Kerry

(Sheet 20) There is an **earthwork** (although not a particularly impressive one) cutting off Doonmore **promontory fort** (V 30 98) a mile and a bit south-south-west of Dunquin. On the site of the fort itself you will find an **ogham stone**.

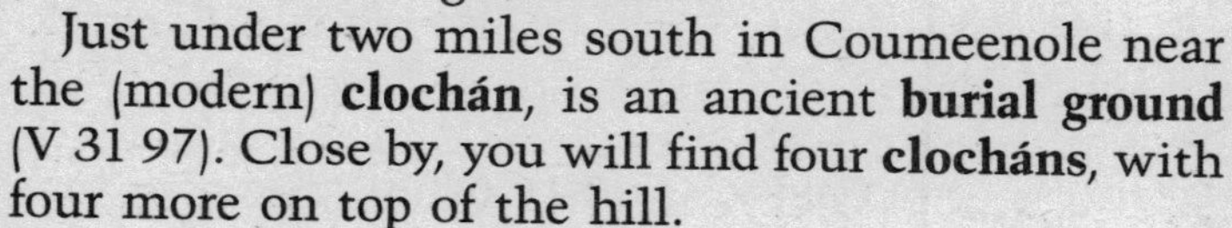

Just under two miles south in Coumeenole near the (modern) **clochán**, is an ancient **burial ground** (V 31 97). Close by, you will find four **clocháns**, with four more on top of the hill.

Easky, County Sligo

(Sheet 7) Finn MacCool, the legendary Irish giant and hero, took it into his head to hurl a stone from Easky into the sea. (See boxed reference below.) Despite his great strength, the stone fell short. In a fit of pique, he struck it with another stone and split it. You can see the results of this escapade by the side of the road to the east of the village. The stone is called, appropriately, **Finn MacCool's Fingerstone** (G 38 38).

Travel just under a mile south to Fortland to find a ruined **court tomb** (G 37 36).

Ennistimon, County Clare

Two miles north of the town near the Derreen River in Ballydeely, you will find a fifty-feet diameter round **cairn**.

Finn MacCool

Finn MacCool was a 1st-century Irish hero directly descended via his mother, Murna of the White Neck, from the mystical Tuatha Dé Danaan. (See boxed reference on page 116.)

He avenged his father by slaying Liath Luachra, a Connacht Lord, and stealing the Treasure Bag which contained various magical weapons and jewellery.

(cont.)

He was sent to learn poetry and science from the sage Finegas who sat by the River Boyne constantly fishing for the Salmon of Knowledge. Finegas eventually caught the magical fish, but Finn promptly stole it and ate it.

Thus fortified, he returned home to be placed in charge of the Fianna (see boxed reference on page 44) by King Cormac MacArt.

Finn married when his hounds brought home a fawn which transformed itself into a beautiful girl. His wife was then kidnapped by the fairies and while searching for her on Ben Bulben, Finn came across a young boy. When the lad mentioned his mother was a deer, Finn realised this must be his own son and named him as Oisin, or Little Fawn.

Finn, who was only moved to tears twice in his whole life (and on one of these occasions he wept for the death of his dog, Bran) met his end at the Battle of Gabhra.

Fermoy, County Cork

(Sheet 22) Travel five and a half miles south-west of Fermoy to the eastern end of the Nagles Mountains. In the townland of Knockaunacorrin, you will find the **Lord's Cairn** or **Carn Thierna** on the top of a small hill (W 73 93) which also shows remnants of a **hill fort**. This is one of several cairns on Nagles peaks. The mountains were traditional gathering places at Lughnasa. Excavations in the 19th century unearthed a food vessel in a chamber within the cairn.

Fethard, County Tipperary

(Sheet 18) If you travel four miles north to the crossroads on the border of Cooleagh and Grange-barry and explore these neighbouring townlands, you are likely to find a number of unlisted **earthworks** and **ring forts** (S 21 41).

Freshford, County Kilkenny

(Sheet 18) Tullaroan village lies about six miles south-south-west of Freshford, with a ruined church to the south-east. If you take this site as your base, you will find a number of **earthworks** and **ring forts** in the immediate vicinity (S 38 56).

Galbally, County Limerick

(Sheet 18) The closest megalith is a **wedge tomb** just a mile north-east in Corderry (R 81 28).

Almost as close, but less easy to reach, is the **cairn** (R 77 28) on top of Duntryleague Hill, a mile and a half to the west of the village. There is also a well-preserved **passage grave** west of the summit.

Galway City, County Galway

(Sheet 14) Like most of Ireland's larger population centres, Galway offers much in the way of cultural and historical exploration. For something a little older, you will have to travel four miles east on the N6 Oranmore road. South of the road are the remains of a Medieval church, where you will find two **bullain stones** and a huge semi-circular **cashel** (M 35 25).

Glandore, County Cork

(Sheet 24) Just under two miles east of the resort, in Drombeg, you will find an impressive **stone circle** (W 24 35) known (almost inevitably) as the **Druid's Ring.** The monument is particularly well signposted, so you should have little difficulty in reaching it. The ring is about 30 feet in diameter and aligned to the winter solstice sunset. Check the large recumbent stone to the south-west for cup marks. Excavation of

the area in 1957 unearthed an urn burial of a young man at the centre of the circle. I have conflicting reports on the radiocarbon dating of this find. One pointed to a period around AD 480 to 720 - well into the Christian era. Since there is no evidence of stone circles still being built at this time, this would suggest that the circle was taken over for ritual purposes by the later Celtic peoples. The other report of the dating gives a figure around the first century BC. But even this seems late when set against the evidence of the urn, which is at most early Iron Age in style and may, in fact, be Neolithic. There were originally 17 stones in the circle and two of them are fairly obvious male and female symbols. One of the tall portal stones to the north-east has two cup marks, one with a surrounding ring. West of the circle is an Iron Age village site (of which little now remains). This originally consisted of huts surrounding a communal cooking pit and hearth. It seems that stones were heated in the hearth, then dropped into the pit to heat water. Archaeologists carried out some domestic experiments which showed the ancients could boil 75 gallons of water in 15 minutes with this device - a rather better performance than my old immersion heater at home.

Across the bridge from Glandore is the village of Union Hall. Just under two miles south east of here, very near the coast at Carrigillihy, are the remnants of a Bronze Age stone **ring fort** (W 22 33). Once it enclosed two tiny homesteads, a model of one of which is featured in Cork Museum. The site seemed little more than a low, oval **tumulus** prior to its excavation in 1950 when the ring wall was discovered, protecting a square house, the remains of which were superimposed on an earlier oval dwelling. (It is this earlier dwelling which is featured in the museum model.) The square house was dated

somewhere between the 6th and 10th century AD, placing it squarely in Christian times. The oval house seems to be of the same date as the surrounding wall, which includes a megalithic **orthostat**. There were both Neolithic and Bronze Age finds nearby. The reluctant conclusion of the experts was that this was an early Bronze Age fortified single farmstead - reluctant because homesteads of this type were not supposed to exist at so early a date.

Glanworth, County Cork

(Sheet 22) In Neolithic times the body of a woman was buried in the inner chamber of what is now generally held to be the largest and finest of Ireland's megalithic **wedge tombs** (R 77 02), while her head was interred in the outer court. You can examine the site of this curious practice at the **Hag's Bed** a mile and a quarter south-east of Glanworth in the townland of Labacallee. Archaeologists have found evidence of at least three further (later) burials here, along with pig, ox and sheep bones and pottery fragments. The tomb itself is so large it approaches some of the gallery graves in the Loire Valley. To the south and south-east are remnants of the kerbing of the cairn which once covered the entire tomb. What covers it now are three capstones, the largest measuring 26 x 8 feet.

A mile south-west of the village in Moneen, look carefully to the west of the road to find a Neolithic **cairn** (R 74 02) which seems to have been built on top of some sort of **ritual enclosure**. The cairn has a diameter of about 45 feet, surrounded by kerbing stones. In the middle you can see the capstone of a **wedge tomb** in which a man and a woman were buried. Excavation of this site produced a rich array of finds including urns, food vessels, potsherds, querns, stone rubbers, an axe-hammer and other

human burial remains. The ritual enclosure on which the cairn was erected is marked by a fosse over 50 feet in diameter and comprises a low mound which yielded up Neolithic pottery and other remains.

Glenamoy, County Mayo

(Sheet 6) There is a ruined **court tomb** (F 82 38) signed as a National Monument, five miles north-west of the village at Ross Port.

An eroded **promontory fort** (F 83 45) stands eight miles north-north-west at Doonvinalla, while eight miles north-west is a **cairn** (F 79 41) in the ancient churchyard of Kilgalligan, among the sand dunes.

Glenbeigh, County Kerry

(Sheet 20) Take the N70 Cahirsiveen road south-west and travel five and a half miles to reach Drung Hill. Beside the road here you will find a **cairn** with an **ogham stone** (V 58 88). It is referred to locally as Laghtfinnan Penitential Station and believed to mark the grave of the parish's patron saint.

Glencolumbkille, County Donegal

(Sheet 3) The scenic beauty surrounding this village is spectacular, possibly explaining why the early saint Columcille founded a monastery here and established a centre of pilgrimage.

There are 15 pilgrim stations in and around the village (G 53 84) visited by pilgrims on June 9, the saint's day and, interestingly for those who are intrigued by the associations between Christianity and the Old Religion, some of them are also megalithic sites.

Ask locally for directions to the stations - it's a three-mile walk to take in them all - and note the following:

Station 1 is the remnant of a **court tomb**. There is a **souterrain** nearby close to the door of the Protestant church, although this is unlikely to have been built earlier than the 9th century.

Station 3 has a **cairn** and three **healing stones** which pilgrims pass around their bodies to cure illness and promote sanctity.

Station 4 has a **ring work** and **cairn**.

Station 5 has a **ring work** and three **cairns**.

Station 8 has three **cairns**.

Station 9 is a **cairn** with a **court tomb** only a quarter of a mile away to the north-west. A small hole has been bored through the centre of the cross on the pillar at this station, through which pilgrims may get a glimpse of heaven. The stone also brings luck, presumably in the shape of fertility, to childless women, an interesting association with megalithic hole stones which are widely reputed to promote fertility.

Station 10 is a **cairn.**

Station 11 is a **cairn.**

Station 13 is a **cairn**.

Station 14 is a **cairn.**

It is now difficult to ascertain exactly which stations have prehistoric elements and which are entirely Christian, but Professor Estyn Evans has remarked that 'at most of these sites, half-destroyed prehistoric monuments, small cairns and cashels, are associated directly or indirectly with pilgrim practices.'

Apart from the stations, Glencolumbkille has several other interesting megalithic sites within easy reach. Less than half a mile north of the church you will find **Munnernamortee Cave** (G 53 85) which is not a cave at all, but the remains of a long **cairn**. The site is an archaeologist's nightmare. A track has been driven through the cairn and walls built. The

chambers of the complex were used to house calves, pigs, lambs and, in one instance, as a grain store. Despite this indelicate treatment, the site is sufficiently unusual to warrant a visit.

Travel the three miles south-west to Malin More, then go a further half mile south at the crossroads to find the first **portal tomb** (G 50 82). Return to the crossroads and go half a mile east-north-east to find another (G 50 83), then a further three quarter miles east-south-east for a third (G 51 82). If not completely overcome and the weather is good, keep going less than half a mile south-south-east to Cloghanmore where you will find a reconstructed **court tomb** (G 51 82). If the weather is wet, you may have difficulties reaching the monument, which is situated in very marshy ground. This is an interesting example of the type with twin galleries at the western end of the court, one of which is roofed with a heavy capstone. At the other end of the court, it is worth very careful examination of the two smaller chambers since their entrance stones are decorated with curvilinear motifs. Unfortunately, however, the designs are so badly weathered they are now extremely difficult to see. If these decorations are contemporary with the tomb, it would suggest a comparatively late dating for Cloghanmore. Much of the tapered **cairn** has survived, although the shape it is now in is not original: it was 'tidied' by 19th-century Board of Works 'experts' who found it originally no better than a huge stone pile which had been used as a quarry.

A half mile beyond this **court tomb** you will find another (G 51 82).

Glendalough, County Wicklow

(Sheet 16) This is an early Christian monastic site (T 12 96) of extraordinary natural beauty which has been tastefully exploited by the Irish authorities as a tourist attraction. As a result there are two excellent car parks (one of which now seems to be run commercially at high season) and a first-class Visitor's Centre with maps, leaflets, a scale model of the site and even a film show.

You can spend a very pleasant day exploring the remnants of early Christian tradition and while there has been no official confirmation of prehistoric habitation, there are some suspicious placements of several boulders on the site and one renovated **ring work** may have marked an older earthen enclosure.

If you take the path south from the cemetery and cross the little bridge over the river, you will reach the **Deer Stone** where, according to legend, a thirsty Saint Kevin, having no cow, persuaded a doe to let him milk her.

Glenties, County Donegal

(Sheet 3) Travel five miles north-west of the village to find Dooey Beach (B 76 01). In the sand dunes along its two-mile stretch is a fallen **pillarstone** known as **Cloch an Stucain**. At Dooey, archaeologists discovered a great many heaps of shells and iron slag, indicative of early habitation. At the lowest occupied levels excavations unearthed a fosse enclosing an area some 130 feet across with various pits. Dating the site has not yet proven possible: to compound the usual problems, it was used as a graveyard probably in early Christian times. One interesting find in the middens was that of the dog-whelk shell. The crustacean was not a food source, but gave up a purple dye used in ornamentation.

Golden Ball, County Dublin

(Sheet 16) Half a mile west of this hamlet on the Dublin-Enniskerry road is Kiltiernan Demesne which houses a superb **dolmen** known as the **Giant's**

Grave (O 19 22). The unusual shape of the 40-ton capstone led to its being described as 'a sphinx-like monster, advancing out of a rocky hill on some half dozen short and rickety legs.' Despite the legs, I think it looks more like the famous shark *Jaws*. Excavations beneath the 22-feet-long capstone unearthed some crude examples of Neolithic pottery. Although a National Monument, this **portal tomb** lies on private property and you should be warned that casual visitors are not welcome.

Gortahork, County Donegal

(Sheet 1) A short distance from Falcarragh, itself close to Gortahork, is Ballyconnell House, in the grounds of which you will find **Ceannfaoladh's Stone** (B 93 33) with its crystalline vein believed to be the fossilised blood of the hero Faoladh, beheaded by the mythic prehistoric giant and wizard, Balor of the Baleful Eye.

Gowran, County Kilkenny

(Sheet 19) There are many magnificent Medieval sights to see in and around the village, but the only great

Balor of the Baleful Eye

The giant king of the Fomorians lived around 2000 BC. He had only one eye which turned baleful when he spied through a keyhole on Druids preparing their spells. From that point on, everything he gazed upon died.

The baleful eye had its uses, however. When the Tuatha Dé Danaan invaded, the ancient Balor was carried out and his eyelid roped open so that he could glare lethally at the enemy.

The Tuatha were the match for his magic, however. Lugh of the Long Arm took aim with a slingshot and not only killed Balor with a stone through the eye, but managed to slaughter the 27 Fomorian warriors ranged behind him.

stone of note lies five miles to the south-west at Tullaherin where, near the base of the round tower in the early monastic site, you can find a fragment of an **ogham stone** (S 59 48).

Granard, County Longford

(Sheet 12) Take the N55 road to Bellanagh a mile and a half north-east to pass across a sector of the **Black Pig's Dyke** or **Dunchhaladh** (N 34 82), an example of ancient engineering. (See boxed reference below.)

In quite a different direction, six miles to the north-west, you will find a worthwhile **portal tomb** in the townland of Aughnacliffe (N 26 88).

Greenan Mountain, County Donegal

(Sheet 1) There is a famous **hill fort** and **cashel** on the top of this mountain known as the **Grianan of Ailech** (C 36 19). The nearest population centre is the city

Black Pig's Dyke

The great forts on the Hill of Tara are reflected in the Emain Macha (Navan Fort) which lies in County Armagh in Northern Ireland and is consequently outside the scope of this Guide.

Some 18 miles south of the Emain Macha, still in County Armagh, is a curious enclosure known as the Dorsey which archaeological evidence suggests dates to the same period as the fort - which makes it at least Bronze Age and possibly earlier.

From the Dorsey a series of banks and ditches, collectively known as the Black Pig's Dyke, runs westwards to the Atlantic coast, crossing the modern Border in the process.

The curious name arises from an ancient legend that a magical pig threw up a furrow (the dyke) from coast to coast in a single night.

of Londonderry just under five miles south-east, across the border in Northern Ireland.

The **ring fort** was known as the sun palace and the site was held sacred up to about AD 1100. Traces of ancient earthworks surround the more obvious construction, enclosing an area of more than five acres and dating to the early Iron Age or beyond. The cashel was reconstructed in Victorian times, but modern archaeologists are doubtful about parts of the inner restoration.

Headford, County Galway

(Sheet 11) If you can drag yourself away from the excellent angling offered by this resort village, it is worthwhile travelling the two and a half miles north to Moyne in neighbouring County Mayo where you will find an old church site enclosed by a **cashel** (M 26 50). This seems to be yet another example of prehistoric holy ground granted a change of use by the Christian Church. Old customs die hard, however. Near the west end of the church are two **pillarstones** through which coffins were traditionally carried.

Hollywood, County Wicklow

(Sheet 16) The village which lies just to the east of the Baltinglass–Dublin road nestles by the first foothills of the Wicklow Mountains. One of the area's most interesting **megaliths**, the so-called **Hollywood Stone**, is no longer there. This **boulder**, inscribed with the mystical labyrinth motif, once stood by an old roadway three and a half miles south-east in Lockstone Upper. Now, however, you have to travel to the National Museum in Dublin's Kildare Street to see it. You can, however, see a less spectacular inscribed **boulder** by the roadside at Wooden Cross on the top of Togher Ridge (O 00 03). To reach it, drive three and a half miles south-east on the L107 to the

road junction, then five miles east-south-east to the ruins of the church at Templeteenawn, then leave the L107 to drive a further two and a half miles west-north-west to reach Wooden Cross.

Take the short road west out of Hollywood to join with the main Baltinglass-Dublin road, turn left at the junction and travel towards Baltinglass keeping an eye out to your left to find the **Athgreany Piper's Stones** (N 93 03), perhaps my favourite **stone circle** in the whole of Ireland. The 14 boulders with their fallen fairy thorn and (possibly) inscribed **outlier** are described again elsewhere in this Guide - check the Index for the reference.

Hospital, County Limerick

(Sheet 18) This curiously-named village draws its name from the Medieval Knights Hospitaller of St John of Jerusalem. This mystical Order may have been drawn to the district by its various prehistoric remains and their heavy encrustation of local legend.

Just a mile and a half west, for example, you will come to Knockainy village nestling to the south-east of Cnoc Aine hill on the summit of which you will find an ancient **cairn** and the remnants of three small **ring barrows** known collectively as **Mullach an Triuir** (R 67 36).

The hill itself marks the seat of the goddess Aine, who was honoured there right up to the latter years of the 19th century. (See boxed reference on page 105.) Village men brought large torches of hay and straw to the summit, then circled Mullach an Triuir anti-clockwise before moving down to the fields and herds carrying the gifts of fertility and luck.

Much the same distance from Hospital in a north-north-westerly direction, you will find a **stone circle** (R 69 38) in the townland of Ballynamona.

Three miles north-east of the village, you will find

Aine

Like so many ancient Irish goddesses, Aine was a member of the Tuatha Dé Danaan. (See boxed reference on page 116.) She became patron goddess of Munster around 1000 BC and was associated with fertility in women and cattle.

Sometime in the 2nd century AD, Aine met up with Ailill Olom, the King of Munster, who was so overcome by her charms that he raped her. Aine cut off one of his ears in the fight, so that he was known as Ailill Bare Ear until she completed her revenge by killing him.

Cromwell Hill, which has less to do with the despised English Lord Protector than with Crom Dubh, the prehistoric harvest deity. (The southern spur of the hill is known as Crom Dubh's Castle.) Explore the hill itself to find remnants associated with the legendary Irish warriors, the Fianna. (See boxed reference on page 44.) These remnants include a **tumulus, ring forts** and a **wedge tomb** (R 73 39).

Three miles south of Hospital you will reach the village of Knocklong. Just south of Knocklong there is a hillside **cairn** (R 72 31).

Howth, County Dublin

(Sheet 16) In the grounds of Howth Castle (worth seeing in their own right for their beauty) you will find **Aideen's Grave**, an interesting **portal tomb** (O 28 39). Although partly collapsed, the megalith remains important if only for the size of its quartzite capstone which, at 70 tons, is the second largest in Ireland after the Browne's Hill dolmen in Carlow.

Two miles south-south-east of Howth Harbour is a **promontory fort** (C 29 36) with ditch and rampart defences, probably dating to the Iron Age. To find the

fort, look out for the Bailey Lighthouse, which was actually built inside it.

Aideen

Aideen was the wife of Oscar, son of Oisin and bravest of all the Fianna. (See boxed reference on page 44.) He was such a fighter that he slew three kings during his very first battle.

Aideen was so much in love with Oscar that she died of grief when he finally met his match at the Battle of Gabhra. Legend states that Oisin buried her on Ben Edair at Howth Head and set a cairn over her grave - an honour usually reserved for kings or great warriors.

Inch, County Tipperary

This is **wedge tomb** country. Half a mile east you will find the remains of one in Knockcurraghbola Crownlands and a much finer example two miles north-west of Shevry crossroads (itself three miles east of Inch) in Knockcurraghbola Commons.

Inchigeelagh, County Cork

(Sheets 24, 21) This Lough Allua resort is set in the heart of megalith country. Only two and a quarter miles west-south-west to the north of the Gougane Barra road in Gortafludig, is a **wedge tomb, Tuama an Mhinistre** (W 19 64). You will find an **ogham stone** on Kealvaughmore Hill about a mile and a half south of this site (W 19 62). Two and a half miles south of the stone in Derryvacorneen is **Bárd an Rú wedge tomb** (W 19 58).

There is yet another **wedge tomb**, **Mearogafin,** four miles west-south-west of the resort in Lackabaun (W 18 63). Two miles south-east of this site in the townland of Clogher, you will find another **wedge tomb** (W 20 61) and a further mile and a quarter on to the south-east is an alignment of five **stones** (W 22 60) in the townland of Farranahineeny.

Seven miles west-north-west of Inchigeelagh via Ballingeary in the townland of Bawnatemple, you

will find what was Ireland's tallest **pillarstone** (W 12 70). Unfortunately, this 19'9" giant toppled in 1985 and snapped in two. By a curious coincidence, the disaster occurred on St Patrick's Day, leading one to wonder if the saint is still trying to rid Ireland of the remnants of her great pre-Christian past. A mile and a half north west of the pillarstone in Keamcorravooly is a **wedge tomb** (W 10 71).

Inishcrone, County Sligo

(Sheet 6) At some point in the mists of history, a member of the celebrated O'Dowd family at Tireragh managed to get hold of a magical mantle which he used to change a visiting mermaid into a wholly human woman. She proved so beautiful in both forms that he insisted on marrying her and together they produced seven children. But the mermaid eventually recovered her mantle, regained her true shape and returned to the sea after petrifying the children in an act of violent revenge.

Should you feel the story to be unlikely, travel just short of two miles south-south-west of Inishcrone to Scurmore where you will find proof - the **Mermaid's Children** (G 27 28) on the north-eastern side of a **tumulus** in the form of seven **pillarstones**.

Kells, County Meath

(Sheet 13) Although a noted monastic centre with a great many worthwhile Christian artefacts and architecture, Kells (shown on the sheet as *Ceanannas*) has little to offer in the way of megaliths. There is, however, an **ogham stone** in Keim Churchyard, Castlekeeran, about two and a quarter miles west-north-west (N 67 76).

Kenmare, County Kerry

(Sheet 20) Find the bridge in this angling resort and look around for the ruin of the 17th century castle known as Cromwell's Fort. From the fort you will find a **stone circle** about 600 yards to the south-west with a **boulder burial** in the middle (V 91 71).

You can see a second similar structure - **boulder burial** surrounded by a **stone circle** - by travelling seven miles east on the L62 to the junction of the rivers, then turning south with the River Slaheny for a further three miles to reach Gurteen just beyond Glanlough to the south west (W 00 69).

Kilcolgan, County Galway

(Sheet 14) This is a **ring fort** centre of almost embarrassing riches. Check your local map to establish the boundaries of the barony of Dunkellin,

then explore within them. You can scarcely avoid finding something of interest - archaeologists have recorded close on 400 **ring forts** of earth and stone in this comparatively small area (M 42 17).

Kilcormac, County Offaly

(Sheet 15) Although there is no longer much to see (except some worthwhile scenery) you may enjoy a short trip three miles north-west to Lough Boora (N 16 17), the site of the earliest known human habitation in the Irish midlands. Excavations unearthed the stonework of a (probably temporary) dwelling used by a hunting and fishing community somewhere around 8000-7000 BC.

Kilcullen, County Kildare

(Sheet 16) Two miles south-west of the town is 600-feet-high Knockaillinne in Knockaulin townland. Your climb will be repaid at its summit by the truly massive **ring fort** of **Dun Aillinne** (N 82 07), the 15-feet-high earthwork which encircles a site of close on 20 acres. Archaeological excavation unearthed Iron Age wood structures although the original site may be older. It is known to have been the royal seat of the Kings of Leinster and there are still traces of ancient roadways to it on the hillside. There is a hilltop **cairn** within the earthwork, dating to the Bronze Age and with evidence of Iron Age use. This structure has been partly destroyed by quarrying and the remains are only a few feet high.

Four and a half miles south you will find in the townland of Kilgowan a **standing stone** and a **stone circle** known as the **Piper's Stones** (N 83 01).

Kildare, County Kildare

(Sheet 16) In the grounds of the Protestant Cathedral, just off Kildare's central market square, is the site of

Sheela-na-Gig

In pre-Christian Ireland - and, indeed, long after Christianity had taken hold - a common charm against infertility was a stone carving of a woman exposing her sexual organs. They appear notably in Irish churches built prior to the 16th century. About 300 of these little carvings, known as Sheela-na-Gigs, survive to the present day.

Some scholars identify the Sheela-na-Gig with the yonic statues of Kali which appear at the entrances of Hindu temples. In her aspect of Kalika, Kali seems to have been remembered in ancient Ireland as Caillech, the Old Woman who gave birth to all the races of men.

The derivation of the term Sheela-na-Gig may draw on the same source as the famous Irish jig, which, in pre-Christian times, was an orgiastic dance.

a pre-Christian Fire Temple dedicated to the Goddess Brid. (The Cathedral itself is associated with St Bridget, the Christian form of the old goddess.) The site (N 72 12) is marked rather tastelessly in modern concrete

Brid

Brid, or Brigid, is one of the more confusing of the ancient goddesses of Ireland. She seems to be the same entity as Dana, who was known as the mother of all the Irish gods except one - the patriarchal god Dagda, who was her father. In Kildare, she is often identified with the 6th-century Christian Saint Brigid, who established a well-thought of monastic community there with the help of a hermit boyfriend from the wilderness of Newbridge.

Associated with blessings and fertility, Brid had three sons, who in turn collectively fathered a single grandson, named Ecne or Knowledge.

with nothing else to see, although you might console yourself by inspecting another pre-Christian survival within the Cathedral building – an obscene little **Sheela-na-Gig** carved on the underside of a Bishop's tomb. (See boxed reference on page 111.)

Kilfenora, County Clare

(Sheet 14) The village lies in the heart of the Burren, an area as notable for its megalithic remains as its unusual flora. (See boxed reference on page 66.) Call at the local Burren Display Centre to buy a detailed large-scale map of the district, otherwise you will certainly miss many of the ancient riches of this unique area.

Use the map as your guide to precise locations, but a good starting point might be to travel north-north-east of the village to the ruins of Noughaval Church. From this point, you will find a number of **wedge tombs** to the north and east with several **chamber tombs** and eleven **ring forts** on the ridge to the south east. One of these, at Ballykinvarga (R 20 94), is more interesting than it looks since it is one of the very few Irish forts ringed with defensive **pillarstones** (known to archaeologists as *chevaux de frise*). You will find the only easy access on the south side where there is a passage through the defences to an entrance. The walls of the fort consist of limestone blocks, some up to five feet in length. Beyond the fort and obviously not part of the chevaux de frise defences is a seven-feet-high **pillarstone** which may have been an earlier megalithic structure.

When you have exhausted the immediate area continue your exploration of the Burren for sight of many more **ring forts** and **megalithic tombs**, including the much-photographed **Poul na Brone Dolmen** (M 23 00).

Kilfinnane, County Limerick

(Sheet 22) The **mound** in the village itself (R 68 22) is likely to be an historical adaptation of an early **ring fort**. There are further **ring forts** and **tumuli** three miles north-east on the western end of Slieve Reagh (R 25 71). A **stone circle** (R 25 73) lies on the eastern slope of the mountain.

Kilkenny, County Kilkenny

(Sheet 19) Although an important Monastic site and of strategic historical importance, this attractive county town has little in the way of megalithic remains. There is, however, an interesting **ogham stone** built into the east gable of Saint Colman's church in Clarabricken (S 57 56), four miles east of Kilkenny. On the top of Freestone Hill, a little less than a mile to the east of the church, is a Bronze Age **cemetery cairn** on which was imposed an Iron Age **hill fort** (S 58 56).

Killala, County Mayo

(Sheet 6) The name of this coastal village on Killala Bay comes from the church founded by Saint Patrick (Cill Alaidh) and a round tower survives from the early monastery.

Four miles drive on the L133 north-north-west via Palmerstown bridge is the **dual court tomb** of Carbad More (G 07 32) with a circular court at each end opening on to a **gallery grave**. Further on at Foghill (three and a half miles north-north-east of Palmerstown bridge) there is a **pillarstone** (G 19 35) said to have been erected by Saint Patrick. And one and three quarters of a mile to the north-east in Ballinlena, north of the ruins of the early church of Kilcummin, is Saint Cummin's grave marked by **two pillarstones** (G 21 37).

In Rooghan, six miles west-north-west across

Brian Boru

Although an actual historical personage - he was King of Ireland from AD 941 to 1014 - Brian Boru achieved such a reputation as a warrior, largely through his defeat of the Norse invaders at the Battle of Clontarf, that he has been elevated to the level of a fighting myth, symbolising Ireland's ancient glory.

Tonrehown bridge, there is a ruined **court tomb** (G 13 34), and a mile further north is a **court tomb** with a curved forecourt, at Cloghabracka (G 13 36).

Killaloe, County Clare

(Sheet 18) Beautifully situated on the west bank of the Shannon, the market town of Killaloe, with its associations with Saint Flannan and his O'Brien descendants, including the famous Brian Boru, is a leading church centre in Munster.

In Ballyvally, one and a half miles north-north-west of the town and close to the river, is **Béal Boru Fort** (R 69 74), a huge **earthwork** planted with trees and heaped over a palisaded **ring fort**. The site was excavated in 1961, indicating that the earthwork was supported by stone in the 11th century.

Killarney, County Kerry

(Sheet 20) The centre of Ireland's most famous tourist area of lakes and mountains, Killarney has some special pleasures for the megalith hunter. Two and a half miles east are the **Seven Sisters** in Lissyviggeen (V 99 90) - a tiny **stone circle** of seven stones within an earthen bank with a pair of **outliers** to the south.

Five and a half miles west of Killarney is a **ring fort** (V 88 92) near the former site of Pallis Castle, ancient seat of Mac Carthy Mór. Continue for a mile and a quarter further to the remarkable demesne of Dunloe Castle where, close to an ancient cemetery, are eight **ogham stones** (V 88 91). Seven of these were found in a **souterrain** at Coolmagort during the last century. Because of their protection from weathering in the souterrain, their inscriptions are unusually clear.

Killinaboy, County Clare

(Sheet 14) Ask directions to Leamaneh Castle, then travel just over a mile south-east to the road junction in Roughaun townland. Just south of the road at this point, you will discover the **Crossineenboy Tau Cross** (R 25 92). This is a fascinating double-headed pillar set in a large boulder which is now part of a field boundary. The two carved heads, joined neck to neck, stare up to the sky. For a long time, this megalith was thought to be a Christian cross pillar associated with the church in Killinaboy. Now, however, a growing body of opinion believes it to be pre-Christian in origin.

Another pre-Christian remnant - although definitely carved in Christian times - is the **sheela-na-gig** above the doorway of a ruined church (R 27 91) about a mile and a quarter east south east of the Tau Cross.

Killorglin, County Kerry

(Sheet 20) Well known for its annual Puck Fair in August, the pagan origins of which are uncertain, Killorglin grew around its Norman Castle. In Kilcoolaght, three miles south, is an **ogham stone** (V 79 92).

Killybegs, County Donegal

(Sheet 3) Near Killybegs are several **court tombs**. The closest, less than a mile west-north-west (G 70 77), is at Cashelcummin. One and a half miles south

of Killybegs is a chambered **court tomb** (G 69 73) beside the road at Drumanoo. In Carricknamoghill, three miles north-north-east is another **court tomb** (G 75 81).

Four and half miles from Killybegs in the opposite direction, west-south-west, are three excavated sites (G 67 75) where Neolithic pottery and flint artefacts have been found. The first, in Bavan, is a remnant of **court tomb**. Only four **orthostats** remain, but excavations in the mid-1960s showed the tomb originally featured a two-chamber gallery some 17 feet long. Pots and stone beads were found within it. To the west in the neighbouring townland of Shalwy is another in a ruined state. The third, in Croaghbeg,

Tuatha Dé Danaan

The Tuatha Dé Danaan were followers of the goddess Danu and such fine magicians that they quickly became seen as gods and goddesses in their own right.

They arrived in Ireland, bearing the Lia Fail, or Stone of Destiny, which became the coronation stone of Irish High Kings at a site on the Hill of Tara in County Meath.

They clashed with the Fir Bolg (see boxed reference on page 36), one of Ireland's aborigine races, whom they soundly defeated at the Battle of Moytura. The Tuatha prospered under the leadership of two great heroes, Nuada of the Silver Arm and Lugh of the Long Arm, but eventually fell to the Milesians at Teltown. (See boxed reference on page 172.)

As befitted a magical people, they neither vacated the country nor died out, but went underground instead to the Fairy Kingdom beneath Ireland's many raths and megalithic monuments. They are especially associated with the great Boyneside tumulus of Brugh na Boinne (Newgrange), and with Dowth and Knowth sites.

the townland west again of Shalwy, is a well-preserved **court tomb**.

Kilmacrenan, County Donegal

(Sheet 1) In Letter, two and a quarter miles east of the village is a large **court tomb** known as the **Giant's Grave** (C 17 20). There are two **standing stones** in the area. The first is just over a mile west of Rathmelton (C 20 21). The second is a mile and a half east south east of Kilmacrenan (C 17 19).

Kilmactranny, County Sligo

(Sheet 7) The townlands of Moytirra, about two and a half miles north-north-west of Kilmactranny, are named for the **Plain of Pillars** (G 80 15) which are famed in Irish mythology as the setting for two victories of the Tuatha Dú Danaan. In Moytirra East is a **court tomb** (G 91 14) with four chambers, whilst Moytirra West has the remains of a round **cairn** with **wedge tomb** (G 80 15) where Beaker pottery was found.

Kilmaine, County Mayo

(Sheet 11) An area rich in **ring works** and small **tumuli**, most famous of which is **Raheenagooagh**, a **ring fort** with **souterrain**, three quarters of a mile north of the village in Raunaskeera North townland (M 25 60).

Kilmallock, County Limerick

(Sheet 17) One mile west at Tankardstown South are the recently excavated (1986) foundations, dating from before 3000 BC, of the oldest **Neolithic house** in Ireland (R 59 28).

Kinsale, County Cork

(Sheet 25) Travel to Ballinspittle, four miles south

west of Kinsale, then a further half mile west-south-west for sight of the enormous **rath** at Ballycatteen (W 58 45). The **earthwork** covers an area of three acres on the south-east of a ridge overlooking farmland. Excavation showed the causeway entrance to the south-east was once defended by a series of wooden gates. Three **souterrains** and several huts were built at the centre and there were clear indications of smelting iron and bronze. The site was occupied right up to Medieval times, but was certainly built much earlier.

Knocktopher, County Kilkenny

(Sheet 23) In Ballyboodan, one mile south-west, is an **ogham stone** (S 52 35).

Lauragh, County Kerry

(Sheet 24) Among the breathtaking scenery of the area you will find the remains of a five-**stone circle** (V 74 58) with a short **row of stones** beside it at Cashelkeelty (two and a half miles west) where there are also the traces of a larger **circle.** Another site, the Canfea **stone circle** (V 70 55) in the townland of Ardgroom, is five and a half miles from Lauragh west-south-west.

Lough Arrow, County Sligo

(Sheet 7) This lough (or lake), some four miles west of Ballyfarnan village, is the site of the **Labby Rock** (G 78 14), often called the 'clown of Irish dolmens'. The capstone of this bizarre **portal tomb** measures 15 x 9 x 8 feet thick and weighs 70 tons. It is almost completely covered by heather and grass. Excavations in the 19th century unearthed remains of a cremation burial. The monument is now built into a wall behind a farmhouse field near the north-eastern end of the Lake.

Lough Gill, County Sligo

(Sheet 7) The **'Irish Stonehenge'** (G 75 36) occupies a hilltop to the north of the Lough (east of Colgagh Lake), screened from view by a conifer plantation.

The name, applied in the last century when the site had certain trilithon-like features, is misleading since the **Leacht Con Mac Ruis** is not a stone circle, but rather the remnants of a remarkable **court tomb**, well over 50 feet in length.

On the lower hillside, you will find a **wedge tomb** and a **ring fort** with **souterrain**.

Lough Gur, County Limerick

(Sheet 18) The lake is the supposed resting place of a famous Desmond Earl, Gerald the Rhymer, whose peaceful slumbers are disturbed every seven years when he rides across the moonlit water.

Apart from its romantic associations, the area boasts a wealth of Neolithic remains, although few are signposted. It is well worth starting off with a visit to the Interpretative Centre by the lakeside at Holycross crossroads, two and a quarter miles from Bruff on the Limerick road.

Taking the Centre as your starting point, you will find **The Lios** (R 64 41), Ireland's largest **stone circle,** half a mile north, to the east of the Limerick road. The site is overgrown, but extraordinarily impressive. A wide earthen bank rings a setting of more than 100 stones creating a circle some 150 feet in diameter. Several of the individual stones are massive in scale – one huge block, hauled to its present position from a mile away, stands a good eight feet above the ground. There is a paved entrance passage to the east, flanked by smaller **orthostats**. Excavation of the site, which seems to have been erected between 2000 and 1800 BC, produced enormous quantities of pottery, but no indication whatsoever of habitation, suggesting some sort of ritual meeting place.

There is a lot to see on this site. In the next field north, there is a 15-**stone circle** in a shallow **earthwork** which encloses a mound. To the south-west, there remain nine stones of what was once a 69-**stone circle**.

Across the main road is a ruined **court tomb** and traces of an **ancient roadway** running between The Lios and the shore.

A walk of about 400 yards to the north-east will take you to the **pillarstone** at the bottom of Ardarghlooda Hill. Continue up the hill - noting the ancient **field walls** - to the **ring work** on the summit. A little distance to the north is a **crannóg** known as **Crock Island,** but be sure to bring your wellies if you plan to visit since the ground is boggy even in the driest season.

Back by the shore is another **stone circle** (find Loughgur House then walk 300 yards to the south-east). Look east from the circle to find a **ring fort**.

You can see Knockfennell Hill a few hundred yards north. On the nearside slope you will find a stone **ring fort,** on the summit you will find a **cairn** (R 64 41). To the east in the valley there are terraces which suggest cultivation in ancient times.

Walk 400 yards to the east-south-east of the valley terraces and you will find remains of ancient dwellings. There is a **pillarstone** due east of these and about 200 yards to the north you will see another **pillarstone** on the hilltop.

Two hundred yards south-east of the first pillarstone is a third. And, if you're not too exhausted, 400 yards south-east of this last is a **stone circle** with a flat, kerbed **cairn** nearby. Archaeological surveys indicate that this cairn contained a number of urn burials.

Along the Carraig Aille ridge to the south are two **ring forts** and other stone enclosures.

South-east of Carraig Aille at Loughgur crossroads is a **standing stone** (R 65 40). Take the road back towards Holycross and after three quarters of a mile

in Loughgur townland, you will see a **wedge tomb** to the south of the road. There were at least a dozen people buried here as well as some important decorated Neolithic ware and Beaker and early Bronze Age pottery.

Orient yourself at the ruins of 15th-century Black Castle on the foot of Knockadoon 400 yards north of the road then travel a further 400 yards to the west-north-west to find a **Neolithic cemetery**.

Excavation showed many **Neolithic** and **Bronze Age dwellings** on the south and west sides of the hill. To the north-east of the hill in a corner of the lake is the **Bolin Island crannóg**.

From the Loughgur **gallery grave** about a half mile to the south-west is a **wedge tomb** known as **Leaba na Muice** to the south of the road.

Lough Knockeenagearagh, County Cork

(Sheet 24) If you have the patience to investigate the boulder-strewn area to the immediate south-west of the lough, you will find (eventually!) an exceptionally interesting **decorated boulder** (V 79 27) with about 24 cup marks, some with associated rings, on its surface.

Lough Nahaltora, County Mayo

(Sheet 11) There is an interesting small **wedge tomb** by the L100 roadside in Shrawee at the north-east corner of the lough (L 79 74). There are a few traces of an associated **cairn**, but the remainder has vanished.

Loughrea, County Galway

(Sheet 15) About two miles south-east of this pleasant market town in Masonbrook demesne in Moanmore East is a 70-feet diameter earthen **ring work** set with seven **standing stones** to form **Masonbrook Stone Circle** (M 65 14). The placement of these stones is

1 Ogham stones, sometimes called Alphabet Stones, like this one near Ballyferriter in County Kerry, are comparatively recent megalithic structures, dating to Christian times.

2 A fine example of standing stones, forming part of a circle alignment south of Crookstown, in County Cork.

3 The twin-headed Caldragh Idol, believed to be a Celtic deity, on Boa Island in Lower Lough Erne. *(See the Guide entry under Pettigoe, County Donegal and County Fermanagh.)*

4 The much-photographed Proleek dolmen near Dundalk in County Louth. This picturesque structure has recently found its way onto a popular design of Irish t-shirt.

5 One of the most spectacular court tombs in Ireland lies near Cliffoney in County Sligo. It was expertly restored in the 1930s after four cremation burials were discovered there.

6 Clown prince of Irish dolmens, the Labby Rock at Carrickglass in County Sligo. *(See the Guide entry under Lough Arrow, County Sligo.)* The odd appearance of the dolmen derives from the fact that its 70-ton capstone is completely bewigged with bracken and grass.

7 An equine archaeologist investigates Haroldstown dolmen, County Carlow, once home to a family of Irish peasants in the 19th century. *(See the Guide entry under Rathvilly, County Carlow.)*

8 Tucked away in a forestry clearing, at Magheraghanrush, is Deerpark court tomb, one of a number of interesting and important megalithic sites in the area. *(See the Guide entry under Sligo, County Sligo.)*

9 The 3,000 year old Lios Stone Circle, at Lough Gur in Country Limeric, the largest in Ireland and a site well worth investigation despite the undergrowth.

10 The desolate landscape at Kilclooney More, in County Donegal, yields up a number of fascinating megalithic sites, including the atmospheric dolmen shown on the horizon. *(See the Guide entry under Naran, County Donegal.)*

11 Not to be missed — Bronze Age rock art on the massive Ardmore decorated stone near Mugg in County Donegal. Some forty cup and ring marks appear on its surface.

12 Reanascreena stone circle consists of thirteen megaliths, all but one still standing. Archaeologists believe they have evidence that this was an important ritual site in Neolithic times. *(See the Guide entry under Ross Carbery, County Cork.)*

13 One of the author's favourite megalithic site, the delightful Piper's Stones at Athgreany, County Wicklow. The thorn tree is a common feature of Irish megalithic sites and is associated in folklore with the Fairy Folk or Little People. *(See the Guide entry under Baltinglass, County Wicklow)*

14 The so-called Druid's Ring, Drombeg stone circle and altar stone in County Cork, aligned to the winter solstice sunset. *(See the Guide entry under Glandore, County Cork.)*

15 The possible remnant of a prehistoric fertility cult, the ornate Turoe Stone was removed from an Iron Age ring fort and placed in its present site in the village of Turoe, County Galway. *(See the Guide entry under Loughrea, County Galway.)*

16 The needle-sharp Punchestown long stone which, at twenty feet, is believed to be the tallest megalith in County Kildare. A cist grave appears at its base. *(See the Guide entry under Naas, County Kildare.)*

17 The unique Burren district in County Clare is home to several of the most important megalithic monuments in Ireland, including Poulnabrone dolmen, a 4,500 year old site which has produced pottery fragments and human remains. *(See the Guide entry under Ballyvaghan, County Clare.)*

18 Poulnabrone is one of the more photogenic portal tombs of the Burren and has attracted the attention of artists and photographers (not to mention an annual host of tourists) worldwide.

19 The capstone of Browne's Hill dolmen in County Carlow is, at 100 tons, the largest single megalith in Ireland. *(See the Guide entry under Carlow, County Carlow.)*

20 The drystone ramparts of the massively impressive Dún Aonghus fort on Inishmore, one of Galway's Aran Islands. The tradition of drystone wall construction is still alive in the west of Ireland to the present day.

21 Dún Aonghus in context. The fort, which is accepted as one of the finest prehistoric monuments in Europe, covers fully eleven acres and must have been virtually impregnable because of its clifftop location.

22 The interior of the great promontory fort of Dubh Cathair on Inishmore in the Aran Islands. This terraced structure with its surrounding chevaux de frise (not shown in this picture) may be the oldest fortress on the island.

23 A standing stone at Tara, County Meath, one of the many megalithic remains on this important hill, once the coronation site of Ireland's kings. *(See the Guide entry under Navan and Tara, County Meath.)*

24 An aerial view of the Hill of Tara in County Meath. Although the various megalithic sites on the hill are not particulary spectacular from the ground, they remain among the most important in Ireland.

25 Excavation at Knowth, one of the great passage tombs in the Boyne Valley, unearthed a large number of smaller satellite mounds, some of which are shown here. *(See the Guide entry under Newgrange, County Meath.)*

26 Excavation of the Knowth tumulus in the Boyne Valley was underway at time of writing so that the interior was closed to the public. Access to some of the satellite tumuli is, however, possible. One shows how the ancient builders troubled to decorate the *backs* of stone blocks which would never be seen by human eyes.

27 Most ancient of Ireland's famous Hollow Hills, the great tumulus at Dowth in the Boyne Valley has been plundered all too frequently since the 11th century. You can climb the mound itself, but the interior is now barred to the public. *(See the Guide entry under Newgrange, County Meath.)*

28 The interior of Ireland's most famous megalithic structure, the tumulus of Newgrange in the Boyne Valley. The perspective makes the central chamber appear much smaller than it actually is and the granite bowl in the centre of the picture is one of the most beautifully proportioned artworks in the world.

29 Controversial restoration work at Newgrange in the Boyne Valley gives it the appearance of a flying saucer landing. Experts are convinced, though, that however modern the site may appear, this is how it actually looked when first built some five thousand years ago.

30 The beautifully-decorated entrance stone, one of many inscribed stones at Newgrange. The spiral motif is believed by many dowsers and psychics to represent energy vortices within the mound.

31 The interior of Newgrange. The photograph is taken looking along the entrance passage along which a ray of sunlight illuminates the womb-like chamber on the morning of the winter solstice.

now questionable since local wisdom suggests they were re-erected at some stage in the past. There is a terraced **tumulus** in the same area believed to have marked a place of ritual assembly. To the south you will find a 300-feet diameter **rath** with the remnants of a **souterrain**.

Only four miles from Loughrea to the north-north-east is the village of Turoe where you will find the famous **Turoe Stone** (M 63 22), removed from its former Iron Age **ring fort** site a few miles away at Kiltullagh. The stone itself, now protected from sheep and tourists by an iron grating, is a domed granite boulder just over three feet high. Probably dating from the 1st to 3rd centuries BC, this beautifully-decorated phallic stone has Celtic-style abstract patterns carved in relief across its surface by a technique known as poking. Experts believe it may be a remnant of a prehistoric fertility cult.

Louisburgh, County Mayo

(Sheet 11) Six miles south in the wild country dominated by Croagh Patrick, find a **wedge tomb** at Shrawee (L 79 74) which the locals honour as a holy well.

Louth, County Louth

(Sheet 8) If you want to see the very **pillarstone** to which Cuchulain bound himself in his final heroic battle, travel two miles east-north-east of the town to Rathiddy, east of the road to Dundalk. The stone here is known as **Cloghfarmore** (H 98 02), roughly translated as Great Stone, and is widely believed to mark the last stand of Ireland's notable mythic warrior.

Cuchulain

When Lugh, the sun god of ancient Ireland, lay with Dectera, the result of their union was a child named Setanta. The boy was fostered to a man named Sualtam near the town of Dundalk. At the age of seven he was sent to the court of King Connor MacNessa to begin his education.

Setanta's adventures began when he killed a dog belonging to a warrior-lord named Culan. Culan forced him to take the dog's place until he could breed a suitable replacement and henceforth, Setanta was known as Cuchulain, the Hound of Culan.

His fighting career began soon after he fell in love with Emer, a daughter of the Lord of Lusc. The girl gave him cause to hope, but not until he had proven himself in battle. To prepare himself for life as a soldier, Cuchulain left for the Land of Shadows and began to train under Skatha, one of the greatest of all Irish warriors.

During the time Cuchulain was with her, Skatha went to war against her rival, Aife. Cuchulain joined in and managed to capture Aife. Like many a victorious soldier, he adopted the sixties adage, made love not war and left Aife pregnant.

Cuchulain proved one of those men destined to have trouble with women one way or another. When he finished his training, he found himself pursued by a lady whose attentions he preferred to avoid and jumped from Loop Head to the cliffs beyond in order to escape her. The woman tried to follow, but fell to the rocks below and her blood stained the sea as far as the Cliffs of Moher. (The point at Loop Head is known to this day as Cuchulain's Leap.)

Over time he developed a curious protrusion on his forehead known as the Loin Laoich, or Light of the Champion, which blazed forth in the heat of battle. Cuchulain himself got heated too. When he fought and

(cont.)

L

killed the Sons of Nechtan, he grew so enraged that he was utterly unable to calm down.

His followers sensibly distracted him with a topless parade of Ulster's most attractive girls, then dunked him in cold water. Three barrels of the water turned to steam before Cuchulain was sufficiently himself to dress in his Sunday best and visit Emer. Since he had now proven himself, she allowed herself to be carried off.

A young man named Connla arrived in Ireland and was killed by Cuchulain following a quarrel. Only afterwards did Cuchulain realise the boy was his own son, fathered on the warrior woman Aife.

Cuchulain's death also came about because of a woman. Queen Maeve of Connacht grew jealous of a bull owned by her husband and determined to find herself a better one. She discovered a magnificent animal owned by Daire, a local chieftain at Cooley in Ulster.

Maeve requested a loan of the beast, offering to sleep with Daire in exchange. (The original epic expresses the bargain delicately, saying that she 'extended him the friendship of her upper thighs'.) Daire proved one of the few men immune to Maeve's undoubted charms and refused. The spurned queen promptly marched on Ulster to take the bull by force.

As luck would have it, Ulster was virtually defenceless at this time since the men of Ulster were under a curse placed by the goddess Macha. As a result, every time they were threatened with attack, they went into mock labour and were unable to fight. Cuchulain's divine heritage left him immune to the curse and he held off Queen Maeve's armies single-handed.

During this unbalanced war, infiltrators managed to steal Daire's bull and drive it to Connacht. Cuchulain fought on until he received a mortal wound. Realising he was dying, but determined to keep the enemy at bay for as

(cont.)

long as possible, he tied himself to an upright pillar where Queen Maeve's forces could see him.

Terrified to attack the great warrior, they held back until, three days later, they noticed a bird land on Cuchulain's shoulder and realised he was dead. As they prepared to advance, King Connor MacNessa's men threw off the ancient curse and swept down to rout the invaders.

For those who prefer their stories to end with all the loose ends neatly tied, it is worth mentioning that Daire's bull killed the bull belonging to Maeve's husband, then escaped from Connacht, but dropped dead on reaching Ulster – a thoroughly unsatisfactory conclusion for all concerned one would imagine.

Macroom, County Cork

(Sheet 21) Find the haunted rock-castle of Carrigaphooca, three and a half miles west of the town, north of the river and south of the N22. The early 15th-century stronghold dramatically dominates the rock home of the malign sprite (pooka) from which it gets its name. Two hundred yards north-east of the castle are the five remaining stones of a **stone circle** (W 29 73).

The monastic site at Ballyvourney (W 19 76), eight and a half miles west-north-west of Macroom is worth a visit. The site itself lies in the townland of Glebe, just under a mile west of Ballyvourney School. Look for **St Gobnet's Grave**, where you will find three **bullauns**. Two hundred yards east of Gobnet's House at the upper end of a small glade, two small mounds mark the sites of Bronze Age **cooking places**. There used to be a circular wooden hut here, a birch-lined pit, a hearth and a stone oven. There is also a **sheela-na-gig** (see reference box on page 111) in the Medieval church. Take the road east-south-east to Shanagloon townland where you will find a further **bullaun** and three **ogham stones**.

Mallow, County Cork

(Sheet 21) Not far from the ruins of Mourne Abbey (an

early preceptory of the Knights Hospitaller) which are almost six miles south-south-east of Mallow, at Greenhill is an **ogham stone** (W 57 91) with the remains of another about 40 yards away. A third can be found at Burn Fort **rath** (W 59 91) a mile and a half further on to the south-east. Go on to Island, a mile north-east from Burnfort village, and you will find the partly-restored remains of a **wedge tomb** within a heel-shaped **cairn** (W 60 90). Little or nothing of the cairn remains, but it was originally about 36 feet in diameter, its edges marked by 16 stones. Cremated human bones were found in a deep pit towards the end of the 20-feet gallery.

Eight and a half miles south-west of Mallow, at Beenalaght, is an 11-**stone alignment** (one fallen) near the summit of Reanthesure (W 48 87). These are massive stones, some of them standing more than nine feet high.

Manorhamilton, County Leitrim

(Sheet 7) There are several **chamber tombs** among the wealth of archaeological remains in these border hills. Two and a half miles south-south-east of the village, at Tullyskeherny, there is a two-segment **gallery grave** (G 89 37) as well as two **court tombs**, one with half a dozen secondary chambers.

You can see a dual **court tomb** at Barracashlaun (G 85 42) by returning to Manorhamilton and travelling three miles north-west.

Millford, County Donegal

(Sheet 1) There is a fine **portal tomb** to be found at Gortnavern, three and a half miles north-north-east of the village and a mile or so short of Carrowkeel village to the north. The monument, known as **Diarmaid and Grainne's Bed** (C 20 31), is located on a farm about a quarter of a mile east of the

Rathmelton road. It stands more than six feet high and there are cup marks on the capstone.

Millstreet, County Cork

(Sheet 21) There are lots of megaliths in the Boggeragh Mountains to the south-east of the village. Two sites, both near the Munster Way, are worth a visit.

A little over five miles south-south-east towards the mountains in Glentane East you can see remains of a **wedge tomb**, a **stone circle** inside an **earthwork** with one **monolith** lying outside and another inside the enclosure (W 27 83).

Another **stone circle** is in Knocknakilla (similar to the large circle east of Lough Gur), five and three quarter miles south-east of Millstreet (W 31 85) near the top of Mushcramore. Beside this circle are two **monoliths** and a low **cairn**.

Monaghan, County Monaghan

(Sheet 8) Five miles south-west of the county town there is a **court tomb** (H 61 25) at Tiredigan. The wedge-shaped **cairn** is more than 100 feet long and the court, opening northwards, covers three quarters of a circle. The facade is well preserved and the portal stones are impressive. The gallery has three chambers.

Monasteraden, County Sligo

(Sheets 7 and 12) This is a village on the western shore of Lough Gara. The lake is scattered with islands, some 360 of which are prehistoric **crannógs,** revealed along with various artifacts and 40 prehistoric dug-out boats when drainage operations lowered the lake in 1952. The crannógs range in age from about AD 500 all the way back to late mesolithic times. Two worth inspection are located at G 75 01 and G 72 00.

The former has been dated to 3000 BC, but was occupied through into Christian times. Bone pins and combs were found here, along with wooden bowls, glass beads and bronze ornaments. The latter is more recent, dating provisionally to about 200 BC. One of the more exciting finds at this site was a wooden box packed with personal ornaments including gold-plated pendants and amber beads.

Less than a mile outside the village to the south-west in the grounds of Coolavin House, at Clogher, there are two accessible **souterrains** inside the restored stone **ring fort** of **Cashelmore** (M 66 98).

Muff, County Donegal

(Sheet 1) In Ardmore, just over a mile to the north-north-east of Muff, to the west of the coast road to Carrowkeel and Moville, there is a huge squared **pillarstone** (C 47 26) some seven feet high and three feet wide with about 40 cup and ring markings engraved on the south-eastern face and one on the north-eastern face. These are fine, typical examples of Bronze Age rock art and make the megalith (which is located in a field behind a farmhouse) well worth a visit.

On the hill overlooking the Abbey at Eskaheen two miles north-west of Muff are the **Niall's Rocks pillarstones** (C 45 27).

Mullinavat, County Kilkenny

(Sheet 23) Lughnasa used to be celebrated every year in July on Tory Hill south-east of this pleasing village in the Black Water valley. Well worth visiting is the very fine **portal tomb** – the tallest in Ireland – at Kilmogue (S 50 28), five miles to the north-west of the village. This one is not easy to find since it is not listed as a national monument and there is no official access to it. It is hidden from the road by high hedges and sits in a field next to a farmyard about half a mile west of the Harristown crossroads. Known locally as **Leac an Scail**, the dolmen has a double capstone design, with the larger of the two capstones set at an unusually acute angle and rising at its highest point almost 15 feet above the ground. The **orthostats** at the entrance are themselves a good 12 feet high.

Naas, County Kildare

(Sheet 16) At Furness, three miles east of Naas beyond the villages of Kill and Johnstown is **Longstone Rath** (N 93 20), in the grounds of Furness House. The great earthen **ring work**, some 200 feet in diameter and up to nine feet high, surrounds an inverted saucer enclosure with the 17-feet high granite **pillarstone** at its centre. Finds from the long **cist grave** excavated beside the stone were of the early Bronze Age (Beaker) period and included the bones of a woman and a wolfhound, some pottery shards and items of ornamentation. Excavation work in 1912 suggested the overall length of the pillarstone (including the portion underground) to be about 21 feet, bringing it close to that at nearby Punchestown which is the longest in the county. The excavations also indicated a fierce fire had burned over much of the interior in prehistoric times, suggesting the enclosure was more likely to have been used as a ritual site than as a fort. Dating of the site is uncertain, but the likelihood is that it was erected around 2000 BC.

(On a purely personal note, Longstone Rath has many fond associations for me. It was the site of several psychical experiments described in my very first book, *Astral Doorways* - also published by HarperCollins under their Aquarian imprint - and

the place where a friend and I experienced one of the strangest phenomena of my life – the appearance of a herd of 'fairy horses'.) Furness is a magical spot, with reports of leprechaun and wood nymph sightings in the copse surrounding the 12th-century church a little distance from the rath. It is also private property and while the church and rath are both listed as ancient monuments, it is only courtesy to obtain permission to visit them.

Further south at Punchestown, home of the annual Kildare and National Hunt Races, three miles from Naas on the Athy road, is the **Longstone of Punchestown Great** (N 91 16). You will find it to the east of the road, a tapering **pillarstone** almost 20 feet high, which also has a **cist grave** at its base. This is the tallest megalith in County Kildare. It was originally set tilted, but fell in 1931 and was re-erected in 1934. Measurements taken while it was on the ground showed an overall length of 23 feet. Experts calculate the weight in excess of nine tons.

A third **longstone** of Wicklow granite is to be found at Craddockstown West (N 91 16), half a mile further on to the south-west, and west of the road. Go on another two and half miles south-south-east to see the **Sillagh Ring**, a mysterious great **earthwork**, which is incomplete either because it was never finished or partially destroyed.

Naran, County Donegal

(Sheet 3) Travel seven miles north-north-west from the tweed weaving centre of Ardara to the little resorts of Naran and Portnoo. At low tide you can walk out to Inishkeel (less than half a mile), the little pilgrims' island with its early Christian associations with Saint Conall Caol.

Two miles inland you can discover remains from a more ancient past. At Kilclooney More, south-south-

east of Naran, and about four miles north-north-west of Ardara, less than a quarter mile to the east of the main road, there is a **court tomb** and two **portal tombs** (G 72 96), one massive and one tiny, standing within a ruined **long cairn** close by. The larger portal tomb has a capstone nearly 20 feet long, almost matching the giant capstone at Browne's Hill Dolmen, County Carlow. Excavations unearthed a few Neolithic pottery fragments here. The smaller of the two tombs is now partially collapsed.

Go on west (or two miles due south from Naran) to Doon Lough where there is a well-preserved stone **ring fort** on one of the islands (G 70 98).

Navan, County Meath

(Sheet 13) The **Hill of Tara** (N 92 59), focus of many heroic legends, lies south-east of the town to the west of the Dublin road. At the summit of the hill is the ancient stone **cairn**, the **Mound of the Hostages**. The cairn which contains a **passage grave** was sealed in the Bronze Age with earth. Archaeologists found the passage grave packed with cremated human bones from as many as 200 bodies from the third millennium BC. For a full description of the many ancient sites on this historic hill, see the separate entry, *Tara*.

Hill of Tara

Known as Teamair or Teamhair in Gaelic, the Hill of Tara was the seat of the High Kings of Ireland from prehistoric times and the capital of Ireland until the 6th Century AD.

The site fell foul of a saint's pique. King Dermot MacKerval violated the right of Saint Ruadan to grant sanctuary, whereupon the good saint promptly laid a savage curse on Tara which quickly brought it to ruin.

Nenagh, County Tipperary

(Sheet 18) Named as the site of one of the principal public assemblies of early Munster, this market town is dominated by the fine Butler Castle (a National Monument), which has some remarkable features.

Four miles away, east-north-east at Rathurles, as the name implies, there is a splendid **ring fort** (R 90 80). The original stone gateposts still lie in the field to the north-east. There are ruins of a 15th-century church inside the fort.

Seven and a half miles west into the Arra Mountains is Portroe, near the Killaloe slate quarries. In Lackamore, two and half miles further on to the south, is a **wedge tomb** (R 77 79). And in Coolbaun, less than four miles south-west from Portroe, on the scenic slopes of Tountinna, are the **Graves of the Leinstermen**, a group of stones (R 78 73).

Newbliss, County Monaghan

(Sheet 8) There are several prehistoric sites nearby. In Garran, under three miles north-east, is the **Giant's Grave portal tomb** (H 60 25). Go on to Tiredigan, three quarters of a mile further north-east, where you will find a **court tomb**. Continue to Cloghernagh, a mile and half north-west from the Lecklevera junction, where there's another **court tomb** (H 59 28). There is a third **court tomb** at Carn (H 61 25), a mile and a quarter south-east of the Lecklevera junction.

Newgrange, County Meath

(Sheet 13) The most famous of all Irish megalithic sites, Newgrange (O 00 72) is situated among many others in the Boyne valley, five miles east of Slane and seven miles south-west of Drogheda. It is, of course, a National Monument and there is an admission charge which entitles you to a guided tour after

which you are welcome to explore the site to your heart's content.

Built about 3100 BC, the vast stone and turf **chambered mound** is about 280 feet in diameter and 44 feet high. The mound is bound by a kerbing of large stones, many bearing beautiful carved designs of spiral, lozenge, zigzag and other symbols. There has been controversy over the startling reconstruction of the white quartz wall (reinforced by a cement backing wall to prevent the mound slipping) on top of the south-east sector of the kerb. This was based on the position of the white quartz layers found outside the kerb during excavations between 1962 and 1975 and is meant to restore the appearance of the monument as it was in prehistoric times. The effect has been likened to a grounded flying saucer and while some experts feel the monument should have been left alone, the restoration has gone a long way towards creating an appealing ambience.

Some distance away are the remaining 12 stones of the great **stone circle** (probably about 34) that once enclosed the mound. This circle was built about 1,000 years later than the original structure, dating probably from the Beaker period.

There is a beautiful triple spiral-carved **kerbstone** in front of the slab which blocked the entrance to the tomb. Above the entrance passage is a 'roof-box', which aligns with the rising sun at the winter solstice, so that the rays touch the ground at the very centre of the tomb. Many of the upright stones along the walls of the 62-feet passage, which follows the rise of the hill, have finely-carved geometric decorations.

Entering the great mound is an unforgettable experience. The passageway is both narrow and low in parts, but reaching the central chamber transforms Newgrange into a monument which is vastly more impressive even than Stonehenge in England.

The cruciform chamber has three recesses and a magnificent 19-feet-high corbelled ceiling. Again, many of the stones are decorated. On the floor there are massive stone basins, one in each of the left-hand and rear recesses and two set on top of each other in the recess on the right. Check the top one - there are two bowl-shaped depressions in its surface and it has exceptionally beautiful proportions. The overall effect of the chamber is one of remarkable - and for me totally unexpected - sophistication.

The bowl-shaped depressions are thought to have held milk, or similar liquids used in religious ceremonial, although similar cup marks on upright stones obviously could not have been used in such a way. An earlier age of archaeologists speculated that they might have been kneelers - a child or small adult might squat in the basin with their knees in the indentation.

Excavations in the central chamber produced the remains of two burials and at least three cremated bodies as well as stone beads, small spheres, pendants and various bone pins.

There are two satellite tombs, one to the east and one to the west of the entrance. Cement posts now mark out what was once a **double circle** 'woodhenge' of wooden pillars, enclosing Beaker cremation pits, to the south-east of the main tomb entrance. The two decorated stones outside the Tourist Office came from Dowth and the one just inside the car park fence from Ballinacrad near Dowth.

A little over a quarter of a mile from the great **cairn**, south-south-east, is a large **tumulus**, 220 feet in circumference and 20 feet high. Another quarter of a mile south-east of the tumulus is another **mound** by the river.

A ten-feet **pillarstone** stands about 450 yards north-north-east of the great cairn and another large

tumulus, with stone kerbing, is about a quarter of a mile north-north-west.

Newgrange gets its modern name from the fact that by 1142, the site had become part of Mellifont Abbey farm. These farms were known as granges and by the 14th century, most of its megalithic and mythic associations had all but been forgotten. The site was known only as the 'new grange'.

In 1688, the property passed into the hands of Charles Campbell, who saw it as a convenient source of stone for roadworks. Eleven years later, while his servants were removing stones from the base of the mound, they found the entrance stone with its engraved spirals. Soon the entrance passage was discovered, as was the internal chamber.

Campbell inspected the find and notified Dublin. Edward Lhuyd, the noted Welsh antiquary, came out to investigate. He discovered two skeletons in the central chamber and concluded the structure was the sepulchre of some great personage and his wife. The modern history of Newgrange had begun.

Dowth

A mile and three quarters from Newgrange north-east, back in the direction of Drogheda, is the great chambered cairn of Dowth (O 02 73). This most ancient of the Boyne valley sites has suffered generations of abuse and more than half the original mound has gone, the stone being taken for road-making and building materials. The Annals of Tighernach tell of Dowth being plundered and burnt in the year 1059, with a record in the Annals of the Four Masters of three great early battles at Dowth and a later burning in 1170. In the last century Lord Netterville of Dowth House built a summer house on the summit of the mound.

While listed as a National Monument, this site is

currently closed to the public and entrances into the mound are barred and padlocked. There is, however, little to stop you walking around the exterior of the tumulus - and if you do so, you will be rewarded by the discovery of two large decorated kerbing stones.

The mound itself has a diameter of 280 feet and is 47 feet high, and it contains two known megalithic structures. The entrance to the main tomb is on the western perimeter. One of the tombs, just inside the kerb of the mound, has a single side chamber opening off a large **circular chamber** with decorations on some of the stones.

The main tomb **passage** is 27 feet long, made of uprights supporting the roof lintels and divided by three **sill-stones**, one inscribed in a similar way to those at Newgrange. The passage leads to a **cruciform chamber** with more decorated stones and the remains of a stone basin. A further series of small chambers lead off an opening in the south-westerly corner of the main chamber.

There is a 70-feet-long **souterrain** crossing to left and right of the main entrance, leading to a series of chambers with a beehive chamber at either end, which recent excavations shows to have been mainly associated with dwellings of the Christian era. The souterrain was probably originally constructed in the first millennium BC when the mound was adapted as the base for a fortress.

South-west of Dowth House, a little over a quarter of a mile east of the great mound, is a **mound** enclosing a small hexagonal chamber, with a corbelled roof, and five cells off it. A quarter of a mile to the east of the house there is an enormous circular **earthwork**.

Knowth

The third of the great passage tombs in the Bend of the Boyne is at **Knowth** (N 99 73), a mile and three

quarters north-west of Newgrange towards Slane. This is also a National Monument with admission charge which entitles you to a guided tour - but not, unfortunately, of the inside at time of writing. Currently, the great tumulus is under archaeological excavation so that only about a third of it is actually open to public viewing. Best estimates aim for a reopening in 1994, but this may not mean interior visits by the public since the entrance passageway is longer than that of Newgrange and no-one is certain that the current reconstruction work will render it really safe for large parties.

The excavations have uncovered layers of change and use down through the ages, often quite independent and ignorant of earlier building work. This is especially noticeable in the case of the passages and **souterrains**. There are four souterrains in all and these were built much later than the two original passage graves, which were probably lost and undiscovered at the time of the later works.

Like the other two great mounds it is 280 feet in diameter with a height of between 40 and 50 feet. It is surrounded by at least 17 satellite tombs, at least one of which you can enter, providing you are not with a large party.

The great mound itself contains two differing tombs which almost meet at the centre. The west tomb is just over 100 feet long, including a lintelled stone passage which bends to the right about three quarters of the way along before rising to the lintel-roofed chamber. The east tomb, by contrast, is like the one at Newgrange, cruciform and with a corbelled roof, the passage and tomb extending to an incredible 120 feet. In the right hand recess a beautifully-decorated stone basin was found along with a unique ceremonial flint macehead. Both tombs include decorated stones and there are fine engraved motifs on many of the mound's **kerbstones**.

Foundations of rectangular houses show Knowth to have been a settlement in about AD 800, and over the next two centuries the Kings of Northern Brega made it their royal residence. The Normans also laid claim to it. In 1175 it was granted to Richard de Fleming, only to be abandoned about a century later.

P.A. O'Síocháin, in his book *Ireland - A Journey into Lost Time*, quotes part of Dr John Donovan's entry for Knowth from his *Survey Letters for Meath* of 1836:

> There was a grave here also broken into by the Danes, who searched and robbed it. There was a tradition in this county that all these moats have caves within them in which bars of gold are laid up, but it would be dangerous to open them as evil spirits are watching the treasures.

He makes the point that the legend of the buried gold had more than a grain of truth in it as these ancient sites were used in later centuries for important burials, often along with costly ornaments and personal possessions. Recent excavations found traces of early cremations and among the grave goods stone pendants and bone pins, as well as later Iron Age burials of the early historic period, but the grave robbers down the centuries left us no Celtic gold.

In Monknewton, about a mile and three quarters from Newgrange and to the east, are the remains of a Beaker period circular **henge**.

Several mounds are still largely unexplored in this great cemetery within the bend of the river. About 30 tombs can be recognised within the area, although this is far from the final tally as recent excavations at Knowth have shown. There are many more showing no trace on the surface, which are waiting to be discovered, as well as unopened mounds yet to be confirmed as passage tombs.

Aongas Og

The handsome young god Aongas, son of Boand, the Boyne river goddess, and the Dagda, father-god of the Celts, fell madly in love with a beautiful maiden who visited him in his dreams. Aongas searched long and far for her but to no avail and so fell sick with longing for his unknown love.

Eventually his father and mother took pity on him and found the girl, Caer of Sid Uamain in Connacht. She lived with her maidens on Loch Bel Drecon at Crot Liach in Magh Femin, in the form of swans wearing silver chains.

Aongas changed himself into a swan and the two lovers flew to Brú na Bóinne (Newgrange), singing such lovely music on the way that all who heard it fell into an enchanted sleep for three days and three nights.

Of all the megalithic sites in Ireland, the Boyne Valley complex has attracted the largest encrustation of myth and legend. There is mention of Newgrange in the very earliest surviving Irish epics, the mythic history of the Tuatha Dé Danaan. (See boxed reference on page 116.)

These Lords of Light, as they were called, lived in Brú na Bóinne (Newgrange) - or rather they lived in a mystic Otherworld to which the great physical mound was only an entrance. In the palace halls of the Otherworld, 'three times fifty sons of kings' lived a life of perpetual festivity, fed by three great trees which were always in fruit and a cauldron from which no company ever went away dissatisfied. It was an eternal realm in which no-one ever died.

The first inhabitants of the mystic mound were Elcmar and his wife Boand, personification of the River Boyne itself. Even the physical river had mythic attributes, since it rose in Segais, the Well of Wisdom and occult knowledge. Segais was surrounded by hazel trees which dropped nuts into the water to create bubbles of mystic inspiration, *na bolcca immaiss*. Every seven years these bubbles would pass into the Boyne and hence might influence humankind.

Elcmar's place was eventually taken by Dagda, the father-god of ancient Ireland. The name means 'good god' and the noted authority T.F. O'Rahilly clearly identifies him as a sun-god in his *Early Irish History and Mythology*. This is an interesting association with the fact that Newgrange is aligned to the winter solstice, but Dagda was also known as Ruad Rofhessa, the god of wisdom.

For 'wisdom' one might well read 'cunning', for Dagda gained possession of Newgrange by sending Elcmar on a day-long errand, which stretched to nine months due to Dagda's magical mastery over time. While Elcmar was absent, his wife Boand was seduced by Dagda, conceived and bore their son Aongas, known as Aongas the Young because he was conceived and born on the same day. (See boxed reference on page 142.)

Martin Brennan makes the interesting observation that while Aongas was born during a magical lengthening of the day at Newgrange, the entrance of the sun's rays into the monument's inner chamber marks the beginning of the lengthening of the days in the yearly cycle of the sun. He sees Aongas as a personification of the daylight, hence an even better candidate than Dagda as a sun god.

The ancient mythologies strengthen the linkage. Aongas approaches his father to request a mound of his own in which to live, but Dagda tells him there is none. Aongas points out that Dagda has granted him a day and a night (magically extended) in Newgrange and argues that since a day and a night

encompass the entire world, then the entire world must be Dagda's actual gift. Dagda agrees and grants Aongas possession of Newgrange itself. The most widely-used reference to Newgrange in the ancient literature is Brú Mac ind Oc, the Magical Land of the Youthful Son. The 'youthful son' is, of course, Aongas.

The mound at **Knowth**, known as **Cnogba**, has mythic associations with Englec. Englec was the daughter of Elcmar by the mistress of Aongas, indicating a direct connection with Newgrange.

The mount at **Dowth**, **Dubad**, has an even more interesting early mythic history. The Druid Bresal, like his priestly counterparts in ancient Babylon, decided to build a mound that would reach all the way to heaven. Bresal contracted the men of Erin to do the construction work and agreed on a single day's pay. His sister then cast a spell which would ensure the sun did not set until the mound was completed.

Bresal, however, committed incest with his sister, breaking the spell. The sun set and Bresal's sister proclaimed that 'darkness (Dubad) shall be the name of that place forever'. Martin Brennan again points out that one of the internal chambers at Dowth is illuminated by the *setting* sun on the winter solstice, marking the start of the longest night of the year – the period of greatest darkness.

Newmarket-on-Fergus, County Clare

(Sheet 17) Three miles north inside the entrance to the grounds of Dromoland Castle which is now a first class hotel, are two **ring forts** and **Mooghaun**, a stone **hill fort** (R 41 70) which covers more than 27 acres.

Three miles east-north-east on the eastern shore of Lough Rossroe at Knocknalappa are the remains of a Bronze Age **crannóg** (R 44 70). The site was excavated in the late 1930s following the accidental discovery of a bronze sword. The archaeologists found a bronze pin, bronze gouge, amber beads, a lignite bracelet and some pottery. Despite this interesting collection, they concluded from other evidence that the crannóg had never actually been inhabited - the finds seemed only to have been stored there and may have originated in other dwellings nearby.

Newtown Cunningham, County Donegal

(Sheet 1) About nine miles north-west of the town on Greenan Mountain is the massive late-Bronze-Age or early-Iron-Age **ring fort** (C 36 19). The thickness of the great walls of the fort contains two galleries and it stands surrounded by three rings of eroded earthen banks.

The site is famous in Irish legend and it was finally wrecked by Muirchertach O'Brien, King of Munster in 1101, avenging the destruction of Kincora by Domnal Mac Lochlainn, King of Aileach 13 years earlier. The fort was restored towards the end of the last century.

Newtown Forbes, County Longford

(Sheet 12) In the ancient churchyard of Cloonmorris, County Leitrim, four miles north-north-west, just inside the gate is an **ogham stone** (N 08 85).

Oldcastle, County Meath

(Sheet 13) The Loughcrew Hills run in a four-mile ridge to the south-east of this small but ancient market town. About 25 miles west of the Newgrange complex, the Loughcrew Hills bear rich traces of a similar megalithic culture (N 58 77), although on a smaller scale.

An interesting common factor between the two sites is the use of white quartz to cover the whole or part of the mounds. At Loughcrew it was recorded in 1856 that the entire base of the large **cairn** 'T' was covered by a two-feet thickness of sparkling white quartz for a height of three or four feet inside the kerb. It is thought that the thickness of the low layer was due to an upper quartz facing collapsing, inferring that the whole mound was covered. Two of the cairns still have names, **Findcairn** and **Carnbane**, both meaning 'white cairn'.

There are thirty **mounds** and chambered **cairns**, a **rath**, a rectangular **earth work** and a **pillarstone** among other ancient remains on the three main heights. There is a quantity of very fine scribings on the stones similar in style to those found in the Boyne Valley although rather less sophisticated and probably predating them.

The **passage tomb** on the summit of Carnbane East is a perfect example of the Irish 'cruciform' tomb layout. All the tombs show variations of the same plan and form the most remarkable passage tomb cemetery outside the Boyne valley. Close by on the northern edge stands a giant inscribed **kerbstone, The Hag's Chair**, six feet high, ten feet across and two feet thick with a hollowed recess on top like a seat.

Two miles east of the Loughcrew Hills on King's Mountain there is an interesting **monolith** (N 62 77) with fine spiral carvings. It is now used as a rubbing stone for cattle and is the last remnant of a chambered **cairn** on the site.

Oranmore, County Galway

(Sheet 14) You can visit Lissroughan, a circular **henge-type earthwork** (M 43 25), three miles away to the east in Mountain West. Two great **monoliths** mark the entrance to the **rath.**

Pallas Grean, County Limerick

(Sheet 18) New Pallas Grean is a village on the road between Tipperary and Limerick. Under two miles south-west of the village is a fine **motte** (R 75 43) at Pallas Grean Old, its name deriving from Grían, the ancient sun-goddess whose Otherworld domain was in Cnoc Gréine. In Longstone townland, three miles west-north-west of Pallas Grean Old, is a ring fort (R 72 46) with a fine 9′6″ tall pillarstone.

Pettigoe, County Donegal and County Fermanagh

(Sheet 3) The Border follows the river Termon which runs through the middle of this angling village near the north shore of Lough Erne. Seven miles south-west (via road bridge) is Boa Island (H 08 62).

There is an ancient burial ground at Dreenan, near the south-west shore of the island, where you will find the famous **Caldragh Idol**, a Janus-headed **carved stone** of twin cross-armed figures, which probably represents a Celtic deity. On the top of the stone is a five-inch cavity which is thought to have been a slot for a missing part of the sculpture, perhaps an antlered headpiece. Nearby is another **carved figure** that originally came from Lustymore Island.

Piltown, County Kilkenny

(Sheets 22, 23) To the north of the village is the magnificent **portal tomb** (S 50 28) of Kilmogue (see Mullinavat, County Kilkenny). Exploration of the countryside surrounding the village may be rewarded by discovery of one or more unlisted **court tombs**.

Quin, County Clare

(Sheet 17) This village off the Ennis–Limerick road is famed for its 15th-century Franciscan Friary, the ruins of which incorporate part of an earlier castle. Travel two and a half miles out of the village, north of Hell Bridge to Toonagh where there is a flat-topped **mound**, **Magh Adhair** (R 44 77), encircled by a ditch and sited in a natural amphitheatre created by low surrounding hills. This is the site where the Kings of Dál gCais and the O'Brien Kings of Thomond were crowned. The fact that this was also a pre-Christian sacred site is evidenced by a **pillarstone** and a small **tumulus**, west of the river. There is a **stone fort** 500 yards south-south-west.

Raphoe, County Donegal

(Sheet 4) There is a fine **stone circle** of 64 stones, **Beltany Ring** (C 25 00), on the summit of Tops Hill, about two miles south of the village. The name suggests that the pagan fire festival of Beltane was celebrated here. (See boxed reference on page 49.) The circle also incorporates a **tumulus** and the site is substantially older than the Iron Age. It has also been disturbed at some time in the (possibly distant) past so that many of the stones, which reach heights of up to eight feet, lean outwards at acute angles. Despite this, there are theories of astronomical alignments in this circle: one stone at least points to the Beltane sunrise. The tumulus may be the remains of a pillaged **cairn** and there are some experts who believe the whole site should really be classified as a **round cairn** with the **orthostats** comprising a kerbing.

Rathconrath, County Westmeath

(Sheet 12) There are several **ring forts** and other ancient remains in the townlands of Ballyglass, Rathrim, Milltown and Kilpatrick to the north of this small village (N 31 53) between Mullingar and Ballymahon.

On the top of Skeaghmore Hill, two miles west of

the village, is **Carraig na Muice** (N 28 54), a rocky outcrop with 'two marks on it made by the Black Pig' – a reference to the mythical animal which created the **Black Pig's Dyke**. (See boxed reference on page 101.)

Rathcroghan, County Roscommon

(Sheet 12) The area (M 80 83) has traditional associations with the Goddess Medb, who presided, like Baccus, over the process of intoxication. Pagan kings of Ireland married the Goddess at the time of their coronations, tossing back flagons of beer to produce the necessary divine intoxication.

(Medb was also Queen Maeve of Connacht, named for the ancient goddess and slain by a son of King Connor MacNessa while she bathed in a lake. See the boxed entry on Cuchulain for further adventures of this intriguing lady.)

The name Rathcroghan derives from *Cruachain*, the extensive limestone plain which stretches from Roscommon to Castlereagh and was once thought to contain an entrance to the Otherworld.

Against such a rich mythic background, it will come as no surprise to learn the district is particularly rich in megalithic remains. Find your way to Rathcroghan Crossroads, then visit the following sites:

Less than 200 yards south-south-west on a knoll beside the road is a **ring barrow** (M 79 83). Some 400 yards further on, you will find a large **ring fort**.

Half a mile south-south-east to the west of the N5 Tulsk road in the townland of Toberrory, you will find a large **tumulus** with a small **ring barrow** on top (M 80 82). A little more than 100 yards away to the north-north-east is **Medb's Lump**, a fallen **pillarstone** commemorating the ancient Goddess.

A further half mile east-south-east of the tumulus,

there is a narrow roadway leading south from the Tulsk road. A little less than 800 yards along this lane, you should find a field path running west to **Dathi's Grave** (M 80 82), sometimes grimly known as the **Hill of the Corpses**, a **tumulus** and **pillarstone** surrounded by an **earthen bank**.

Three hundred yards west of Dathi's Grave are the remains of a stone **ring fort** and **souterrain**. A further 250 yards north is a further **ring work** while 300 yards north-west you will find the **Cave of the Cats** - the actual entrance to the Otherworld - which features a **souterrain** and two **ogham** inscriptions. A few yards to the north-west is a **ring barrow**. Four hundred yards south-west you will find two linear **earthworks**, one of which will take you all the way to **Manannán's Fort** a stone **ring fort**.

Rathdrum, County Wicklow

(Sheets 16, 19) About three and a half miles south of the village in an area known as the Meeting of the Waters, you will find the demesne of Castle Howard. The mountain behind the castle is Cronebane on the summit of which you will find the **Mottha Stone** (T 20 83), used by the giant hero Finn MacCool for gaming. (See boxed reference on page 90.)

Manannán MacLir

As his name implies, Manannán was the son of Lir, the ancient Irish sea-god, and subsequently became a sea god in his own right.

He was specifically associated with the Isle of Man, to which he gave his name (and, incidentally, the well-known symbol of that island - Lir had three legs and moved by rolling like a wheel).

Rathfarnham, County Dublin

(Sheet 16) Although a residential suburb of Dublin City, Rathfarnham nestles in the shadow of the Dublin Mountains and is an excellent staging post for robust hiking trips.

Three and a half miles south-south-west, through Rockbrook, you will find a **portal tomb** (O 12 24) in the Mount Venus demesne. The tomb is not in a good state of preservation but is worth seeing, if only for its capstone, which lies against one of the portal stones. When erect, the whole structure must have stood more than 15 feet high. You reach it through a gap in the hedge beside the golf course, about a quarter mile east of Woodtown road junction.

Four miles south-south-east by way of Whitechurch are the remains of Larch Hill **chamber tomb** (O 14 23).

Rathvilly, County Carlow

(Sheets 16, 19) About a mile and a half north of the village to the east of the N81 Baltinglass road in Broughillstown is a grooved **pillarstone** (S 87 83).

Two miles south-east, you will find the **Six Fingers** which, despite its name, is a single **pillarstone** (S 91 79), reputed to creep down to the river for a drink. The stone was thrown there from Eagle Hill, near Hacketstown, by Finn MacCool. (See boxed reference on page 90.)

Three and a half miles south-east of the village to the south of the road, you can inspect Haroldstown **portal tomb** (S 90 77). I have always thought this to be one of the most attractive of Irish dolmens, a view apparently shared by a family who lived in it during the 19th century. They weatherproofed the side stones with mud and turf, but there are no real indications that they interfered with the overall structure, except possibly for the removal of a side

stone to make an entrance. The internal chamber is larger than most - 13 feet long and up to 9 feet wide; no smaller than some urban bedsits. The tomb is pleasantly located on the bank of the Derreen River and very easy to find - simply ask directions to Acaun Bridge.

Four and a half miles east-south-east in Tombeagh is a **pillarstone** (S 93 80).

Rear Cross, County Tipperary

(Sheet 18) This is an excellent centre for megalith spotting, particularly if you are prepared to do a little hill walking.

Just a mile and a half south of the junction in Shanballyedmond, is an interesting **court tomb** (R 84 58). Excavation has uncovered six cremations and more than 30 timber posts linking with the horns of the frontal court.

A mile and a half north-east, you will find a **pillarstone** (R 86 60) with a **wedge tomb** close by to the south. A second **pillarstone** on the site is now unfortunately long gone.

If you travel just short of four miles east to Anglesey Bridge, you are oriented to visit two interesting sites. A mile and a half south-west are the remains of two **wedge tombs** (R 87 57). There is another (minus its roof) two miles north-east of the bridge (R 19 59) and well worth a visit on account of its size.

Rinvyle, County Galway

(Sheet 10) If you are staying in the Rinvyle House Hotel, close to the small beach at this promontory you will find a **chamber tomb** (L 65 63) a mile and a half to the west, near the ruins of the 15th-century Rinn Mhil Castle.

Two miles south-south-east, look for the high

ground south-west of Lough Tully where you will find an alignment of six **pillarstones** (L 67 62). Nearby are the remains of a **stone circle**.

Riverstown, County Sligo

(Sheet 7) Just over three miles south-east is a kerbed **cairn** in the townland of Heapstown (G 77 16).

(While not a megalith, you might like to visit Lough Nasool (G 79 17), two miles east-south-east. It is reputed to dry up every 100 years, possibly due to its association with the dreaded mythic wizard warrior of prehistoric Erin, Balor of the Baleful Eye. (See boxed reference on page 100.)

Roscrea, County Tipperary

(Sheet 15) Just under six miles south-east of this busy market town is an enormous collection of **standing stones** - some 300 in all - at Timoney (S 20 84).

It is a local tradition that these are the result of Medieval land clearance, but since eight form a partial **stone circle** this seems unlikely.

Ross Carbery, County Cork

(Sheet 24) The resort itself is at the head of Ross Carbery Bay where the tides produce Cleena's Wave, one of only three magic waves in the whole of Ireland. (See boxed reference to the Blarney Stone on page 60.)

Just over a mile south-east of Ross Carbery, on the lawn of a private house at Burgatia, is an eight-feet tall **pillarstone** (W 30 35) heavily decorated with some forty **cup marks**.

A mile and a half east is the **stone circle** (W 30 36) at Bohonagh. (See entry under 'Bohonagh' for details.)

Two and a quarter miles east of the village (beyond the remains of St Fáchtna's Church) is a **stone circle** (W 31 37) with a cremation in the shallow grave at the centre. An **outlier** to the south-east has cup marks

as has the capstone of the low **portal tomb** to the east-south-east. There is a second **portal tomb** 500 yards south.

Three miles north-west of the resort at Reanascreena South is a **stone circle** (W 26 41) of 13 megaliths surrounded by an **earthwork**. The circle consists of 12 **orthostats** and has a diameter of about 30 feet. The low earthen bank which surrounds it places this circle in the category of the great henge monuments. Archaeological investigation in the early 1960s produced evidence that the site had been visited by a great many people over a long period of time, suggesting ritual usage, probably as long ago as Neolithic times. There was also a **cremation burial** in a pit within the circle. Another **stone circle** (W 26 44) may be found two miles further on to the north-north-west. From the second circle, you can find a third by travelling a mile and a half north-north-east.

Rush, County Dublin

(Sheet 13) There is a large **promontory fort** (O 27 56) two miles north-east in Drumnagh.

Saggart, County Dublin

(Sheet 16) On the north-east of Saggart Hill (O 03 24) above this ancient monastic site, you will find a complex and interesting **ring work** which includes ditch, ramparts and **tumulus**. There is also a **cairn** in poor enough condition. (See under **Dublin**.) Two miles south of Saggart village is a seven-feet high **standing stone** with five **cup marks** on its southern face.

Scattery Island, County Clare

(Sheet 17) The remains on this Shannon estuary site (Q 97 52) are mainly monastic, dating back to the 6th-century foundation by Saint Senan. There is, however, an indication of earlier usage in the remnants of the **ring fort** which surround the site. Incidentally, the earth from **Senan's Bed**, a stone enclosure, is believed to be an insecticide.

Scull, County Cork

(Sheet 24) This remote and delightful fishing village has the unlikely distinction of housing a planet-arium – one of the only two in Ireland. On a more down-to-earth level, a journey of little over a mile along the coast road flanking Toormore Bay will bring you to a well-preserved **wedge tomb** (V 85 30) overlooking the sea. The tomb is known locally as a megalithic altar and the townland in which it is situated is named Altar in consequence. The tomb has lost almost all the covering cairn and some of its **orthostats**. There are two capstones (one slipped from its original position) and the 12-feet long gallery is open at both ends. A well across the road - still in use - is traditionally associated with the megalith.

Slightly less than four miles west, in Carriganine, is a **portal tomb** (V 86 32). A mile or so further on, you will reach the ruins of Dunmanus Castle (V 84 33) which is sited close to a **boulder burial** - although you will only be able to visit the latter at low tide.

If you are sufficiently intrepid to make the 13-mile trip to Mizen Head, the southernmost point of Ireland, you will find the **promontory fort** of **Dún Locha** (V 72 26) to the north.

Shercock, County Cavan

(Sheet 8) Travel three miles north-north-west to the townland of Corgreagh (which actually takes you into County Monaghan) to find an interesting **long cairn** (H 70 08). The capstone of the internal chamber has been displaced.

Shillelagh, County Wicklow

(Sheet 19) Travel five miles west-north-west and orient yourself with a visit to the 12th-century Church and Saint Finnian's Cross. Then journey south for a further two miles, to find on the high ground of Moylisha a **wedge tomb** (S 93 67) which has lost its roof.

Sixmilebridge, County Clare

(Sheet 17) Ask the way to Knappogue Castle, which lies about two miles north-north-east of the village. Near the castle you will find a **wedge tomb** (R 48 63).

Skibbereen, County Cork

(Sheet 24) Three and a half miles north-west of the town, there is a large **cairn** with satellite **ring barrows** hidden in a conifer plantation on a hilltop at Skeagh (W 07 36).

Slane, County Meath

(Sheet 13) Slane village is a fascinating historical site and the scene of a recent disaster when Slane Castle burned down. Its owner, Lord Mountcharles, is currently making vigorous fund-raising efforts for reconstruction.

Five and a half miles north-west of the village, you will find a **chamber tomb** (N 88 79) in Rathkenny townland. This megalith is particularly interesting on account of the scribing on its capstone.

Sligo, County Sligo

(Sheet 7) This historic cathedral town lies within easy reach of several megalithic sites, including one in the town itself. East of the Medieval Friary at the housing estate of Abbeyquarter North, you will find the remains of a **cairn** (G 69 36).

Travel just two miles out of the town to the west-south-west to find the Carrowmore Group of megalithic sites which includes **chamber tombs**, **court tombs**, **passage graves**, **pillarstones**, **ring forts** and **cairns** (G 66 33). Close on 100 ancient monuments were originally present on this extensive site which reaches across Tobernaveen, Carrowmore, Graigue and Cloverhill. Academic vandalism in Victorian times has left fewer than 40 sites still worth a visit, but the atmosphere of the area remains quite extraordinary. When you do visit, you will notice several examples of what appear to be **stone circles** but are, in fact, the massive kerbing stones of **cairns** which have now disappeared. Swedish archaeologists have given a tentative dating for the site sometime prior to 4000 BC.

A trip to Cummeen, two and a half miles to the west of Sligo, takes you to another (much smaller) site of **cairns** and other monuments, including an earthen **ring work** surrounding the remains of a roofless **court tomb** (G 65 36).

Four miles west-south-west takes you to Knocknarea mountain at the summit of which is the massive pyramidal **cairn** known (like several other sites) as **Medb's Lump** (G 62 34). The cairn is some 35 feet high and a full 200 feet wide at the base. Local tradition has it that this is the tomb of Queen Maeve of Connacht, but it is certainly far older than this historical figure and may actually be associated with the Tuatha Dé Danaan goddess of the same name. (See boxed reference on page 116.) The cairn itself has never been excavated, but the best guess of experts suggests it may be a **passage tomb**. There are seven other **tomb** sites in the immediate area, including one particularly interesting **passage tomb**. A further passage tomb is sited in Grange North, on the eastern spur of the mountain.

Four and a half miles east north-east (south of the Manorhamilton road) you will find Deerpark and a forestry clearing in which there is a **court tomb** (G 75 36) with roofless galleries. In the neighbouring field to the south is a stone **ring fort** and **souterrain**. Another field south and you will find a **wedge tomb**. In the same area there is a **stone circle**. When you have explored these antiquities, travel two miles north to Formoyle to see the **Giant's Grave** - what is left of another **court tomb**.

Stepaside, County Dublin

(Sheet 16) Just over two miles south-south-west of the hamlet on the south-eastern slope of Two Rock

Mountain, you will find the **Giant's Grave** a **wedge tomb** (O 18 22) a few hundred yards west of the Glencullen road.

Stradbally, County Waterford

(Sheet 22) Travel two miles south-west of the village to Island townland for sight of a fine **ring fort** (X 35 95). Inside the fort (which may once have housed a monastic community) is a **bullaun** and an **ogham stone**.

Swords, County Dublin

(Sheet 13) Two miles out of the town westward, north of Knocksedan bridge is a large **tumulus** known as **Brazil Moat** (O 16 56).

Tara, County Meath

(Sheet 13) This low hill (N 92 59), close to Kilmessan and within striking distance of Trim, Navan and Bective is, after Newgrange, probably the best-known ancient site in Ireland. It lies a mile west of the Dublin-Navan road and is particularly associated with the prehistoric goddess Medb. It was the coronation place of Ireland's most important pre-Christian kings, who mated (symbolically!) with the goddess during the *Feis Temrach*, a ritual banquet.

There are a great many megalithic remains on the hill, so leave aside enough time to explore them thoroughly. Among the sites you will see are:

A **standing stone** near Adamnan's Cross west of the church.

The **Fort of the Synods**, an **earthwork** dating back almost 2,000 years which encompasses (to the west) an even earlier **burial mound** known as the **King's Chair**. Excavation showed timber houses once stood at the centre of the fort. A group of British Israelites decided several years ago that it also housed the Ark of the Covenant and vandalised much of the earthwork as a consequence.

To the south of this fort is a second, known as the **Fort of the Kings**, enclosed by ditch and bank, only part of which now survives. To the north of the

enclosure you will find the **Mound of the Hostages**, a **tumulus** which covers a 4,000-years-old **passage grave**. This was also the site of the coronation stone (**Lia Fáil**) of the Tara Kings, according to local legend. What is believed to be this same stone, a **pillarstone**, now marks a late 18th-century grave within the earthwork. The two minor **earthworks** near the centre of the fort are known as the **Royal Seat** (east) and **Cormac's House** (west). (See boxed reference on page 50.) Note that to the north of the latter, the outer bank swings around a pre-existent prehistoric **burial mound**.

The large **ring fort** south of the Fort of the Kings is known as **Loighaire's Fort.** To the north-west you will find two **ring works** known as the **Sloping Trenches**, while to the east of these is a **ditch** and **bank** enclosing a **burial mound** named for the goddess Grainne. (See boxed reference on page 86.)

Lia Fail

An ancient manuscript entitled *The Magical Stone of Tara* tells how High King Conn of the Hundred Battles went at sunrise to the Ri Ráith at Tara, accompanied by three Druids and three poets.

He was accustomed to making this journey for the purpose of watching the stars 'so that no hostile aerial beings should descend upon Ireland unknown to him'.

On the morning in question, he stepped on a stone which shrieked so loudly that the scream could be heard across the whole of east Meath. Fascinated by this phenomenon, Conn asked his Druids what the stone was called and where it came from.

After 53 days, the Druids returned to him with the news that the stone was called Fail, or Destiny, and that it came from the mystic Island of Destiny.

The **hill fort** on the next hilltop south of Tara is called **Rath Maeve**, a name associated with the matron goddess of the whole site, Medb.

Thomastown, County Kilkenny

(Sheet 19) Visit Legan Castle two miles north-west of the market town to see an **ogham stone** (S 56 42).

Tipperary, County Tipperary

(Sheet 18) Seven miles west-north-west of the county town you will reach the townland of Longstone, a name which suggests that a megalith cannot be very far away. In this instance, the megalith is a **pillarstone** surrounded by a **ring work** (R 80 39).

Tory Island, County Donegal

(Sheet 1) Visiting the island requires a boat trip from Magheraroarty and is worth the effort if only to see the **promontory fort** to the east of the island (B 87 45). Legend has it that this was once occupied by the dark wizard Balor of the Baleful Eye. (See boxed reference on page 100.)

The monastic remains at West Town include some **cursing stones** (B 85 46), last used in anger (so far as I know) against rate collectors in 1884.

Tralee, County Kerry

(Sheet 20) A mile east of the county town you will find an **ogham stone** (Q 85 14) inside the ruins of the peculiarly named Ratass Church.

There are two further **ogham stones** three miles east-north-east (Q 88 15) in the grounds of Chute Hall. This is not, however, their original site, as they are known to have come from near Smerwick Harbour, County Kerry.

Tramore, County Waterford

(Sheet 23) Just two miles west-north-west of this popular resort you will find Carrickavantry **wedge tomb** (S 56 02).

Three miles north there is a **passage grave** (S 59 15) in Carricklong.

Tuam, County Galway

(Sheet 11) Since the megalithic sites of Ireland have long been associated with the activities of the Fairy Folk, it would be a gross omission from this guide if the **Muileann an Liupracháin** (M 42 54) was not mentioned. This limestone cavern lies about two miles north of Tuam to the east of the bridge. The name translates as Fairy Mill and at one time corn was left there for the leprechauns to grind . . . with what result I have no idea.

Four and a half miles west-south-west of the town on the limestone plain are a number of **ring barrows** (M 37 48), two of which were excavated in 1937. The larger contained a cremation burial and a knife. The smaller had a similar burial and a bronze razor.

Five miles west-south-west of Tuam in the townland of Knockmaa several small hills are crowned with **cairns** (M 36 48). In this area, the fairies fought to decide whether Ulster or Connacht would be blessed with good crops, although I can find no record of which side won.

Tullamore, County Offaly

(Sheet 15) Find the church at Rahugh, five miles north-east on the Tyrrelspass road. Two hundred yards to the south-west is an **inscribed boulder** called **St Hugh's Stone** (N 37 31). The inscription is in the form of a ringed cross, which may not necessarily be Christian. This is a particularly useful outing if you are feeling under the weather, since the stone cures headaches.

Tullow, County Carlow

(Sheet 19) The pleasant market town is set on the River Slaney, but if you can drag yourself away from the salmon fishing, there are some interesting megalithic sites within easy reach.

Less than two miles south-east, for example, in the townland of Rathglass (S 86 70), you will find two **pillarstones**, one of which has an **ogham** inscription.

Three miles to the south-south-west in the townland of Ardristan (S 84 71) you will find two **pillarstones** in neighbouring fields. The larger of these stands nine feet high and has six vertical grooves radiating downwards from the top to finish about two and a half feet above ground level. Almost certainly this grooving is artificial: similar grooved stones dating to the early Iron Age are to be found in Brittany. Continue south into the next townland, Aghade (S 84 69), to find both a **portal tomb** and the **Cloch an Phoill**, a **pillarstone** pierced by a circular hole. About a mile south-south-east of this stone is another **pillarstone** distinguished by a vertical grove cut in the eastern face (S 85 68). Follow the Slaney round to Ballynoe where you will find on the eastern bank two further **pillarstones** and a **portal tomb**. Interestingly, the capstone has a groove similar to that on the Aghade pillarstone.

Four miles east of Tullow beside the old Shillelagh road is an enormous four-ringed, stone-built **hill fort, Rathgall** (S 90 72), dating back to at least 700 BC. There is a second, smaller **ring fort** to the north (S 90 73).

Four and a half miles south-south-west of Tullow is the low, conical Ballon Hill (S 82 66), which was excavated in the 19th century to produce an uncommonly fine collection of food vessels and urns. A bronze dagger was also found, as were several **cremation burials**. Records of the dig indicate it was

carried out at 'large and curious entrenchments' known locally as the Walls of Troy, possibly the **cairn** which may still be seen there.

Tulsk, County Roscommon

(Sheet 12) Three miles north-west of Tulsk is Rathcroghan (M 80 83), royal seat of the Kings of Connacht. The hillock here features the most conspicuous of many **earthworks** in the area, reputed to have been the residence of Queen Medb, the goddess who married King Ailill of Connacht. There is a small **standing stone** on the side of the hillock. The limestone cave situated nearby is reputed to be the mythical **Cave of Cruachu** (M 79 83), an entrance to the Otherworld. A quarter mile south of Rathcroghan is a circular enclosure known as **Relic-na-Ri**, with several small mounds within it.

Two miles south-south-west of the village is the **Hill of the Cairns** (M 78 82), coronation site for the Kings of Connacht. A few hundred yards south-east of the hill you will find the **Dumha Shealga tumulus**.

Valencia Island, County Kerry

(Sheet 20) A bridge means that you can reach Valencia (V 43 78) without the need to resort to ferries. Once on the island, make a point of visiting the principal resort of Knightstown to the east. Once there you can travel two miles west-north-west to Cromwell's Fort on Fort Point, inside of which you will find a **pillarstone** (V 40 78).

Two and a half miles west-south-west within the anchorite ruins at Cool East, there is an ancient tomb and **ogham stone** (V 40 75). A second **ogham stone** lies south of the road.

Bray Head, to the south-west, has on its southern slopes the remains of five **clocháns** (V 32 72).

Ventry, County Kerry

(Sheet 20) Your nearest monument is the **Leaba an Fhir Mhuimhnigh**, a **wedge tomb** only about half a mile north east of the village on Caherard Hill (Q 39 00).

A mile north-north-east at Kilcolman is an **ogham stone** (Q 38 01). The same distance north-west in Rahinnane, you will find a **ring fort** (Q 37 01) surrounding a ruined castle.

To the west of Ventry Harbour the lower slopes of Eagle Mountain (V 33 97) once sported a wealth of

ancient remains, including **ring forts**, **pillarstones**, **souterrains**, and literally hundreds of **clocháns**. Many have failed to survive official and unofficial vandalism, but a visit to this area will still prove exceptionally rewarding - leave enough time to explore thoroughly and equip yourself with a good local map, for there remains a great deal to see.

Waterford, County Waterford

(Sheet 23) Although there is much to see and do in this busy little city, there are relatively few megalithic sites within easy reach.

Just over two miles to the south there are the remains of a **portal tomb** (S 60 08) in Ballindud.

A much more impressive example of a **portal tomb** (S 57 16) can be found four miles to the south-south-west in Knockeen. The uprights of the dolmen stand easily nine feet high and there are two capstones (a peculiarity of several tombs in the area). Overall the monument reaches a height of about 12 feet.

Five and a half miles south-west of the city, you will find yet another fine **portal tomb** (S 54 07) in Gaulstown, with an interesting **pillarstone** about a mile to the south (S 54 05) in Ballymoat.

Also worth visiting (although its prehistoric credentials are somewhat suspect) is **Colm's Stone** (S 52 15), some six miles to the north-east, near the ruins of Kilcolumb Church. The stone carries the imprint of the good saint's head and knees, not to mention the remnants of his mystic powers, since you can cure your headache by laying your head in the depression.

Waterville, County Kerry

(Sheet 24) There are a good many megalithic sites within easy reach of this attractive angling resort.

Less than a mile east-south-east you will find the ruins of Templenakilla church with a group of four **pillarstones** (V 50 65) to the north-north-east on a ridge overlooking the road. The stones themselves are up to 10 feet tall and the overall alignment stretches some 30 feet. There is a distinct possibility that these stones are only the remnants of a much more complex site. Careful examination shows traces of an enclosure and some sort of tomb. This would dovetail with the local tradition that the site is the burial place of Skeena, wife of Amairgein, chief poet of the Milesians. (See boxed reference below.)

The lake shore at Beenbane, about a mile to the

Milesians

The Milesians were the last tribe to invade Ireland and became the ancestors of today's Irish people. A preliminary invasion was led by the warrior Ith, but the main horde swept in under the leadership of their king, Mile.

The invaders, who originated in Egypt and reached Ireland via Spain, defeated the indigenous Tuatha Dé Danaan (see boxed reference on page 116) so decisively that they retreated to a subterranean kingdom beneath their raths **and** dolmens, **turning into Fairy Folk in the process.**

Mile named the new Milesian homeland Scotia, in honour of his wife, Queen Scota, and the name remained in use until the 12th century. Later the country was divided into two zones of influence, each with its own Milesian chieftain. When one died, the other, a warrior named Eber, ruled from Tara as the first High King of Ireland.

north-east, has an interesting **ring fort** with **souterrains** (V 51 66). When you find it, explore the fields to the north for a scattering of ancient remains.

If you can find a boat to take you to Church Island in Lough Currane, about two miles east-north-east of Waterville, you will find two **pillarstones** in the ruins of St Fionán's Church (V 53 66).

Approximately four miles to the south in Loher townland are a number of stone **ring forts** (V 50 61).

Westport, County Mayo

(Sheet 10) Two and a half miles east-north-east of this busy market town, just off the N60 Castlebar road, is an interesting **tumulus** set on top of a hill (M 03 84).

About four miles out of Westport on the T39 Louisburg road at Killadangan there is a four-**stone alignment** (L 94 82) in a low-lying field to the north of the road. Although not particularly difficult to reach, despite the waterlogged nature of the area, the alignment is very inconspicuous - its largest stone is no more than four feet high - and easy to miss. Nevertheless, it is well worth the effort since there are also the remains of a **stone circle** and several **pillarstones** nearby, making this a potentially important excavation site for archaeologists.

Some four and a half miles south-south-west you will find **Saint Patrick's Chair** (L 96 78) which, despite the Christian associations, is a **cairn**, the stones of which feature some interesting cup and ring marks.

Wexford, County Wexford

(Sheet 23) Wexford bills itself as a Medieval city and has many historical attractions. I can find no megalithic sites in the immediate area, but ask directions to Ferrycarrig Heritage Park (T 01 23) less than three miles west-north-west of Wexford, where

you can see some interesting reconstructions of Stone Age (and later) buildings.

Wicklow, County Wicklow

(Sheet 16) There is an **ogham stone** five and a half miles south of the town by the roadside in Castletimon (T 29 86).

Epilogue for Eccentrics

There have been some very odd discoveries at megalithic sites in recent years. They were made not by archaeologists - although some archaeologists were involved - but by groups of individuals from both scientific and non-scientific backgrounds, bound together only by the belief that there were megalithic mysteries which went well beyond the usual ancient grave/ritual site type of explanation.

Two formal studies in particular have been instrumental in producing quite unpredictable results. One is the romantically-named Dragon Project, founded in London in 1977. The other is the somewhat more recent Gaia Programme.

The studies examined megalithic sites throughout the British Isles, including Ireland. Although badly underfunded, preliminary results attracted the attention of a few academic establishments who were moved to supply specialist - and often expensive - scientific gear.

Over a period of years, Geiger counters (for measuring radioactivity), magnetometers, ultrasound detectors, scintillation counters, electro-magnetic field recorders, infra-red cameras and various other pieces of equipment have been used on megalithic sites. Some of the results obtained have been startling.

At the megalithic 'tombs' on Baltinglass Hill (County Wicklow), for example, radio signals emanate from the monuments, detectable in specific, clearly-defined areas.

Newgrange, by contrast, and one of the cairns at Loughcrew, have both exhibited the curious property of blanking out radio transmissions, including background noise.

Elsewhere, ultrasound detectors operating in the broad 25–80kHz band have shown certain stones emit an ultrasonic click at sunrise and sunset, with a more generalised ultrasound pulse appearing intermittently at several sites.

Radiation readings at megalithic sites produced even more exciting - if somewhat bewildering - results. It has long been recognised that our environment is a sea of radiation, composed of energies from beyond the planet (mainly, but not exclusively solar), energies generated by the Earth itself (from, for example, radioactive decay), and various electromagnetic energies associated with human activity, such as radio and television broadcasting, electricity supply, etc. Collectively, this energy soup is known as *background radiation*.

There are some sites which give radiation readings higher than background and others, notably in Cornwall, where the readings are lower. The implications of this latter discovery are fascinating. They suggest, in effect, that the stone circles measured are acting as a ring shield against radiation. The effect is not subtle. Measurements taken in the summer of 1985 showed Geiger readings were actually halved by the shield. Three years earlier, a steady drop in background radiation was noted at a site as a thunderstorm approached - directly opposite to what one would reasonably expect.

At one circle, the Merry Maidens in Cornwall,

measurements showed defined areas with above-background radiation levels, and neighbouring areas below background. Until the measurements were taken, such an effect was held to be impossible - and remains impossible in relation to current scientific theory.

In some instances, the effects associated with the megaliths have been so pronounced that they required no more delicate instrument than the human eye to record them. A stone in the western sector of the Rollright Stones in Oxfordshire showed dramatic short-term magnetic anomalies during a survey in 1983 and three years later produced a visible electric 'flame' which, while short-lived, was successfully photographed by investigator Paul Devereux.

Virtually all the megalithic sites examined show what might be called dowsing effects. That is to say, certain of the stones are aligned to underground water courses and 'energy tracks' discernible through the use of dowsing rods. While it is unlikely that you would wish to invest in electronic measuring equipment - or lug it around on your travels, come to that - there is no doubt at all that dowsing, which requires only inexpensive, highly portable equipment, can substantially increase your enjoyment of a megalithic investigation.

Almost anybody can be taught to dowse. Yet most people find it impossible. This is because almost everyone who tries to learn starts out with the traditional forked stick. But the traditional forked stick is very difficult to use - so difficult that failures are common. Dowsing rods are far easier: so much so I could almost guarantee you will find yourself able to use them if you follow the instructions in this section of the Guide.

Your first step is to make yourself a set.

To do so, all you need is two wire coathangers (the sort they use to send back the dry-cleaning) and a pair of wirecutters.

Step One, start with your basic wire coathanger

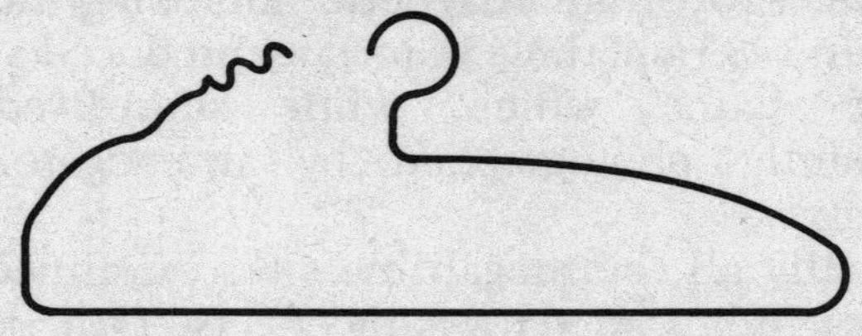

Step Two, untwist, so that it opens out

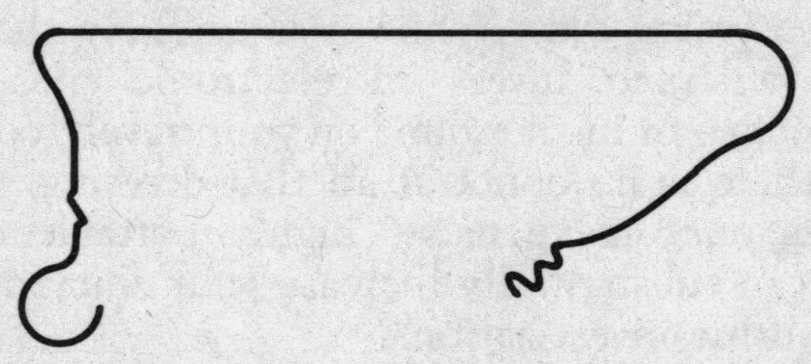

Step Three, bend into a rough L-shape

Step Four, use wirecutters to trim the ends

Untwist the wire at the join and pull apart slightly so you are now looking at the ruin of what was once a perfectly good coathanger.

Next, bend what you have into a rough L-shape. As you do so, you will discover that what you have is a reasonably good L-shape in the middle, with messy ends.

Use your wirecutters to trim off the messy ends and you will be left with one nicely formed L-shaped wire rod. Ideally, the shorter leg of the L should be a little longer than the width of your hand.

Repeat the same procedure with your second coathanger and you will end up with a set of dowsing rods, like this:

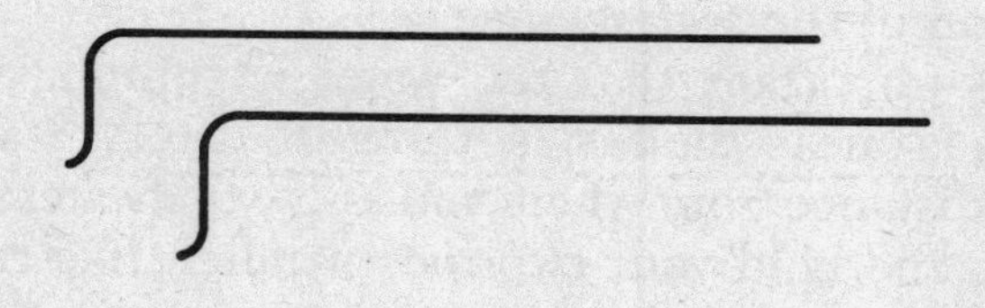

And simple though they were to make, these are the finest, most sensitive, easy-to-use dowsing rods you could own. Their design was first brought to my attention by an old school friend, Don Anderson, who had found sections of the British Army using them to detect both waterpipes and watercourses.

Another friend, the Dallas-based publisher Steve Peek, a veteran of the war in Vietnam, told me U.S. troops had used them to find land mines in preference to the sophisticated electronic detectors issued by the Army.

To use the rods, hold each one loosely by the short leg, like this:

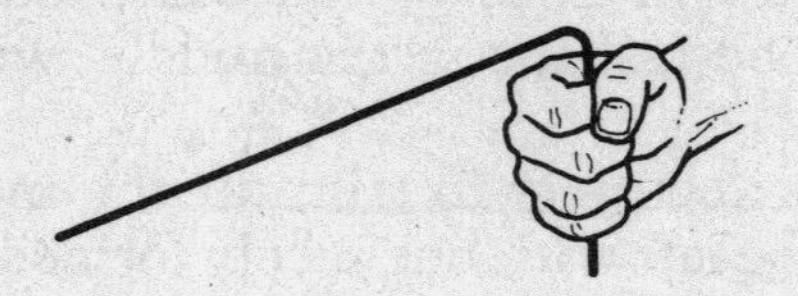

They should be able to swing easily, left and right, so a light grip is important.

Becoming a dowser takes a little practice, but not much. The best place to start is on any piece of land where you know there is an underground stream or watermain. Ideally, you should know the exact location of the watercourse.

It is important that the water is running water, which is one of the easiest things to detect. Start out some distance from where you know the watercourse to run and hold your two rods parallel, like this:

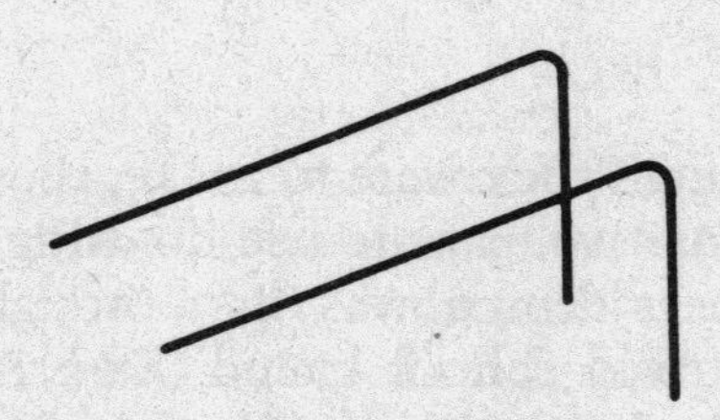

Grip them loosely, exactly as shown in the first illustration. Now, tucking your elbows in to your sides and moving slowly, walk in a line that will take you across the underground watercourse, roughly at right angles.

As you cross the stream or pipe, you will find that the two long arms of the rods swing slowly inwards and cross.

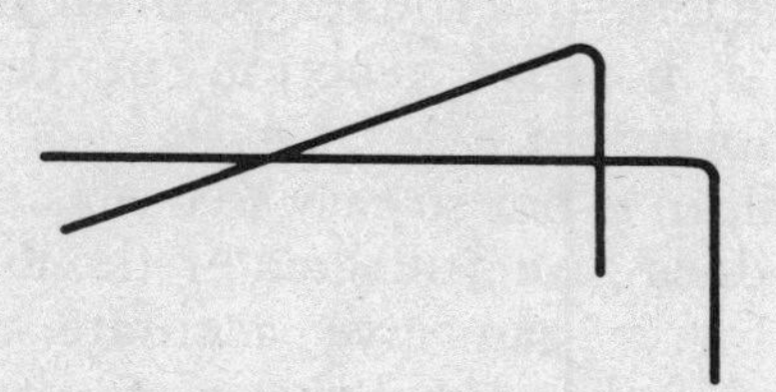

No effort on your part is needed. Hold the rods loosely, walk slowly, and they will swing and cross entirely of their own accord.

Your next step is to try to detect underground water in an area where you do not know its location. The simplest way to experiment is to go to the home of a friend and try to detect the route of their watermain where it connects with the house. Your friend can let you know afterwards how accurate you were.

A second useful piece of equipment is a dowser's pendulum. This is even easier to put together than your set of dowsing rods. All you really need is a small weight and a length of thread. Metal beads work well for the weight since they have a ready drilled hole for the thread to pass through.

Try to avoid using thread with a twist. It tends to start your pendulum spinning and so distort the swing. This rules out most of the cotton in the family sewing box, which, if you look closely, is made up of finer strands twisted around each other.

Nylon thread, which is stronger, is often a single filament without a twist - fishing line is especially good.

When you first make up your pendulum, use at least a yard of thread - two yards if you have it. This is probably more than you will need in practice, but it allows you to 'tune' the pendulum. To do so, walk slowly over your chosen site holding the pendulum and adjust the length of the thread until you find you are getting a positive reaction in the form of pendulum movement.

The pendulum is not so easy to use as the dowsing rods, but it does give you greater flexibility. Some dowsers claim it can give accurate answers to questions about the megaliths: a steady to and fro swing indicates a positive response, a circular motion denotes a negative answer. (One dowser cautions that the positive/swing and negative/circular motion depends on the energy field of a particular area. So check by asking the pendulum an obvious question, e.g. is this man male/is this man female? Whichever way the pendulum moves for each answer is then the correct response.)

In Ireland, one of the best places to test your megalithic dowsing abilities is the environs of the so-called Druids Stones at Blarney Castle, in County Cork. You will notice that many of the trees growing near the circle have twisting, corkscrew branches - a phenomenon dowsers claim is related to spiroform earth energies. Whether or not this is true, dowsing reactions in this area are the strongest I have ever experienced.

Select Bibliography

Achill, Kenneth McNally, David & Charles, Newton Abbot, 1973.

Antiquities of the Irish Countryside, Seán P. Ó Ríordáin, Methuen, London, 1987.

Erinsaga, Jim Fitzpatrick, De Danann Press, Dublin, 1985.

Exploring West Cork, Jack Roberts, Key Books, Skibbereen, 1988.

Irish Mythology, Peter Kavanagh, Goldsmith Press, Newbridge, 1988.

Prehistoric and Early Christian Ireland, Estyn Evans, B.T. Batsford, London, 1966.

Riddles of the Stone Age, Jean McMann, Thames & Hudson, 1980.

Standing Stones and Other Monuments of Early Ireland, Kenneth McNally, Appletree Press, Belfast, 1984.

Tales of the West of Ireland, Gertrude M. Horgan (ed.), Dolmen Press, Dublin, 1975.

The Archaeology of Ireland, Peter Harbison, Bodley Head, London, 1976.

The Shell Guide to Ireland, Lord Killanin and Michael V. Duignan, Gill & Macmillan, Dublin, 1989.

The Woman's Encyclopedia of Myths and Secrets, Barbara G. Walker, Harper & Row, San Francisco, 1983.

Index